AF211918

REUTLINGEN

European School of Business

Timo Priester

An Analysis of the Philippine Retail Structure

A Survey for GfK Asia Pte., Ltd (Philippines)

Schriftenreihe des ESB Research Institute

Herausgegeben von Prof. Dr. Jörn Altmann

Band 37

SCHRIFTENREIHE DES ESB RESEARCH INSTITUTE

Herausgegeben von Prof. Dr. Jörn Altmann

ISSN 1614-7618

Timo Priester

AN ANALYSIS OF THE
PHILIPPINE RETAIL STRUCTURE

A Survey for GfK Asia Pte., Ltd (Philippines)

Schriftenreihe des ESB Research Institute

Herausgegeben von Prof. Dr. Jörn Altmann

Band 37

ibidem-Verlag
Stuttgart

Bibliografische Information Der Deutschen Bibliothek

Die Deutsche Bibliothek verzeichnet diese Publikation in der Deutschen
Nationalbibliografie; detaillierte bibliografische Daten sind im Internet
über <http://dnb.ddb.de> abrufbar.

∞

Gedruckt auf alterungsbeständigem, säurefreien Papier
Printed on acid-free paper

ISSN: 1614-7618
ISBN-10: 3-89821-693-4
ISBN-13: 978-3-89821-693-7

© *ibidem*-Verlag
Stuttgart 2006
Alle Rechte vorbehalten

Printed in Germany

Acknowledgements

I would like to take advantage of this opportunity to express my gratitude to the people who supported me during the completion of this master thesis. My greatest thanks go to Mr. Vu the Du, General Manager of GfK Philippines, who gave me the possibility to write my thesis in cooperation with GfK Asia. He was an excellent supervisor during the whole time and his contributions to the results of the project have been essential. I am really pleased Mr. Vu the Du is the second examiner of the thesis. Above all, I appreciate he is always game for a personal chat, especially during having Starbuck's Coffee.

I am further deeply indebted to the first examiner of the thesis, Prof. Dr. Detlef Vogt from Reutlingen University. Prof. Dr. Vogt gave me the opportunity to write this thesis at the European School of Business in Reutlingen and supervised the project. I particularly want to thank him for his valuable comments, suggestions and criticism, which enabled me to improve my work considerably.

I also want to show my gratitude to the staff of GfK Philippines: Gev, thanks for organizing a perfect trip for me. Raimond, Chel and Anna, thanks for introducing me into the Philippine mobile market. Angel and Christine, I am grateful you showed me the world of Philippine home appliances. Michael and Vince, thanks for letting me know about the audio visual market. Francis, thanks for informing me about the Philippine retail business. Without the enormous help of all of you, I would not have been able to manage this thesis. Besides your professional input, thanks a lot for integrating me into your team so quickly. I really enjoyed our common time in the Philippines!

Last but not least, I would like to thank the numerous proofreaders, whose contributions to this final version cannot be overestimated. These are Mr. Axel Blasinski, Miss Nina Kariadis, Mr. Fabian Lorenz, Mr. Elvis Mutseura, Mr. Maik Priester, Mr. Jens Radstaak, Mr. Max Richardson, Mr. Thorsten Stumpp, Mr. Nicolai

Urbaniak, Mr. Gary Wieczorek, Miss Beate Ziegeler and especially Miss Sikiu Alejandra Campero Arandia. Thank all of you so much for your time and help!

Management Résumé

This thesis was written in collaboration with GfK Asia Pte., Ltd. (Philippines). Its topic is the analysis of the Philippine retail structure. Three different business markets of the Southeast Asian archipelago have been evaluated: The mobile, the home appliance and the audio visual market. The main objective has been to create Philippine Matrices for each market. These matrices are summarizing tools that reflect the local retail structure by displaying information about the total number of shops in a certain market. They are subdivided according to the retail shop type, the shop size and the distribution channel **(see chapter 1)**. The theoretical background of this dissertation consists of an overview about relevant marketing concepts (such as market forms and product planning, **see section 2.1**) and basic principles of retailing (including retail institutions and retail environment, **see section 2.2**).

After the enactment of the Retail Trade Liberalization Law in 2000 **(see section 5.3)**, the Philippines began to open its business markets to foreign investors. Since the country with its 87 million inhabitants virtually started going global, the industrial progress has been substantial. In September 2004, the GfK Group, the fourth biggest market research institute worldwide with headquarters in Germany, set up a subsidiary in Manila, the Philippines dominant capital **(see section 4.6)**. The GfK Group provides clients from industry, retail, media and the service sector with information services. This includes details about sales, stocks and distribution of products, from which analyses e.g. on sales volumes and market shares can be derived **(see section 4.3)**. GfK has built up special panels that enable the company to track the data regularly from a representative sample of retailers. Based on the GfK Methodology, the results can be projected to the universe of all retailers in Manila. The consolidated information is finally sold to the manufacturers **(see section 4.4)**.

The typical Filipino retailer is different from the German one. Generally, independent retailers are distinguished from organized ones **(see section 5.1)**. Especially independent shops often only have a few square meters and are equipped very basically. They are usually crammed with merchandise, which gives the impression they are crowded and hard to overlook. The bigger and well-ordered organized shops look more European and attract a more sophisticated clientele with a higher purchase power **(see section 5.2)**. The market structures of the Philippine retail trade are quite unstable. Many shops are not registered and are run illegally, mainly due to reasons of tax evasion. These circumstances have unpleasant implications for GfK Philippines, since many retailers are not willing to let their sales be audited. High dropouts are recorded, which are incompatible with data accuracy **(see section 5.4)**. A series of interviews with shop owners have been conducted to gain information about Filipino retailers. They were questioned about various topics such as their customers' demands, the influence of the Chinese market and the mutual competition among the retailers **(see section 6.1)**. A summary of these results is given in **section 6.2**.

The Philippine Matrices for the mobile market reveal a total of 1,042 mobile retailers in Manila **(see section 7.2)**. There are almost five times more independent retailers than organized ones (863 to 179), which corresponds to a percentage of 83% to 17%. However, the numerical superiority of independent retailers is not reflected in their sales volumes: The market share for independent shops is only slightly higher than for organized (55% to 45%, **see section 7.3.1**). The Philippine mobile market is very dynamic. In a positioning matrix with the underlying dimensions "stability" (stable versus unstable) and "style" (modern versus conservative) it can be classified as very modern and very unstable **(see section 7.3.2)**.

GfK currently tracks three Major Domestic Appliances of the Philippine home appliance or white goods market: Refrigerators, washing machines and air-conditioning. Compared to the greater provinces, the market penetration for white goods in Manila is considerably higher **(see section 8.1.2)**. The distribution of independent and organized shops is the opposite of the mobile market. The Philippine Matrices show 250 home appliance shops in the 12 million-capital, from which 80% are organized **(see section 8.2)**. These 80% of organized shops hold a corresponding market share of 80%. The home appliance market is characterized as conservative and stable. In the positioning matrix introduced above it is classified opposite to the mobile market **(see section 8.3)**.

GfK audits data about six electrical appliances in the Philippine audio visual market, among them televisions, DVD players and camcorders **(see section 9.1.2)**. The total number of shops in the audio visual market is 443; 232 are independent and 211 are organized (52% to 48%). It is the only one of the three studied markets with a well-balanced ratio of shop types (see the Philippine Matrices **in section 9.2**). The average market share for audio visual products is 72.5% for organized retailers, leaving 27.5% for independent ones. Thus, the former shop type holds a disproportionate market share. In a positioning matrix, the audio visual market takes up a place between the oppositely positioned mobile and home appliance market. It is regarded as medium stable and medium modern **(see section 9.3)**.

Since the Philippine subsidiary of the GfK Group just opened 12 months ago, the company still needs to enhance its market awareness and persuade new retailers to join the GfK panel. For this purpose, management recommendations concerning the recruitment of retailers and the application of marketing communications measures have been presented **(see chapter 10)**. While recruiting retailers, GfK is recommended to underline the resulting short- and long-term advantages in order to illustrate the mutual benefits of cooperation. As relationships play an important role in the Philippine business world, it is indicated to develop amicable relations with the (decision-making) shop personnel. Several visits should be planned for each client for this to happen.

In order to enhance GfK's market awareness, the company is advised to engage in classical advertising (e.g. print and online advertisements, brochures and booklets). GfK should further participate at fairs, trade shows and exhibitions, and use Manila's numerous shopping malls to hold company presentations and set up information points. For public relations and publicity, GfK should create press kits, company magazines and engage itself in sponsorships. The company could also invite interested parties to open-door events. Finally, GfK is recom-mended to make use of direct marketing. The company could offer regular (E-) Newsletters and send e-mails to capture the attention of potential clients.

Table of Contents

GfK

List of Tables

GfK

List of Figures

1. Introduction

The Philippines belongs to the newly industrializing economies of Southeast Asia. Since the enactment of the retail trade liberalization law in March 2000, the archipelago began to open its business markets to foreign investors for the first time in the country's history. Since then, the free trade with neighbouring as well as western countries has increased continuously. The Philippines' industrial advances have also been substantial. The Southeast Asian group of islands has finally overcome its isolation, by which it had been characterized for a long time. Well aware of the emerging entry possibilities to the country's huge business markets, GfK Asia, a subdivision of the internationally active GfK Group with Headquarters in Germany, took the chance and expanded its business activities to the Philippines. In September 2004, the market research company opened its first subsidiary in Manila, the capital of the country's 87 million inhabitants.

GfK's business is about market information. The company's aim is to provide clients from industry, retail, media and the service sector with information services. GfK mainly offers information about sales, purchases, stocks and distribution of individual items and derives analyses e.g. about market sizes and sales volumes of certain products or brands. In order to be able to examine the markets of a country, GfK needs specific information from the local retailers. Therefore, the GfK Group has set up retailer panels, through which it receives the data on a regular basis. Currently, the GfK panel consists of more than 150,000 retailers worldwide. The collected data are analysed and finally sold to manufacturers in form of special reports. For organizational decision-makers, these data form the basis for research and development, production planning, distribution and marketing.

This master thesis deals with the organization of the retail structure in the Philippines. It has been written in collaboration with GfK Asia Pte., Ltd. (Philippines) and presents a survey for the company. Because of time and budgetary restrictions, investigations had to be limited to the capital Manila. To this day, assumptions about the retail structure outside the country's dominant metropolis can merely be made on a hypothetical basis. GfK recently began to monitor the retail trade of major cities south of the Philippines, like Cebu and Davao.

It is one of GfK's objectives to preserve and enlarge its retailer panel, but in order to apply the GfK Methodology (see section 4.4) to obtain accurate market data, GfK first needs to know the number of retailers in the various Philippine markets. Therefore, an analysis of the country's retail structure is essential for the company's success. According to this assumption, a comprehensive examination of the retail structure organization of three Philippine markets has been conducted. These were the Mobile Market, the Home Appliance Market and the Audio Visuals Market (see chapters seven to nine). The main objective of the analysis was to create *Philippine Matrices* for each market. A Philippine Matrix is a matrix that displays information about the total number of shops, which sell a certain product type in a certain market. The expression Philippine Matrices is a fixed term used by GfK that refers to the studied markets. The matrices are subdivided according to the following parameters:

- retail shop type
- product type sold / the market
- shop size
- distribution channel.

By defining the Philippine Matrices as summarizing tools that reflect the local retail structure, their usefulness for GfK Philippines becomes evident. Without comprehensive knowledge of the number of shops of each market, a well-founded evaluation and realistic market comments cannot be guaranteed. Since this information is the core of the GfK reports, the importance of the topic of this work is underlined.

This thesis is divided into eleven chapters. The second chapter provides the underlying theoretical background and contains market overview, market forms, strategic product planning and basic principles of retailing. The third chapter "The Philippines" provides general information about this Southeast Asian archipelago. Special emphasis is laid on the economic and political situation of the country. Chapter four is entitled "The GfK Group" and describes the business activities of

Germany's biggest market research company, the GfK Methodology and facts and figures about GfK Asia and its subsidiary in the Philippines. Chapter five contains a report about local characteristics of the Philippine retail structure. The following chapter "Interviews with Philippine Retailers" presents the results obtained from a series of interviews conducted with several retailers. Chapters seven to nine contain the analysis and evaluation of the Philippine Mobile Market (chapter seven), the Philippine Home Appliance Market (chapter eight) and the Philippine Audio Visual Market (chapter nine), including the discussion of the resulting Philippine Matrices. Chapter 10 consists of recom-mendations for the GfK Management and chapter 11 contains the bibliography. Appendix A shows the interview guide; Appendix B contains the choice of given answers. The bibliographical references are given at the end of each chapter. They include recommendations for further reading.

2. Theoretical Background

This chapter contains the theoretical background of this work. The first part provides a brief overview about markets, market forms and strategic product planning. The second part presents basic principles of retailing. There is a special focus on retail institutions and the retail environment.

2.1 Markets and Product Strategy

As already mentioned before, this thesis analyses three Philippine business markets. To encourage the understanding of the realized evaluation, the following includes some basic information about business markets and strategic planning processes taking place within them.

2.1.1 Definitions and Market Forms

Although the usage of the term *market* is widely spread, experts keep on debating about its main definition. A concrete *market system* is a place where buyers and sellers meet and commit to trade. It is agreed that markets are complex economic, social and technological systems that are crucial to everyday life. It is also agreed that yet while we constantly experience markets our understanding of them remains partial and fragmented. Markets are seen through different lenses by many different disciplines. Economists were the earliest to theorise about them and their notions of what constitute markets and how they operate have tended to dominate the prevailing discourse. Marketing academics have taken a comparatively limited view of markets as they see every market as inextricably linked to the notion of segments[1].

Zikmund and d'Amico[2] define market as follows (quotation, p. 8): "A market is a group of potential customers for a particular product who are willing and able to spend money or exchange other resources to obtain what they value in the product offering". The authors also claim that the term market might sometimes be confusing, because it can simultaneously designate various things such as places (the Jade Market in Beijing), buildings (the Fulton Fish Market), institutions (the stock market) and stores (the supermarket). However, for each definition a common ground can be found, as there are always people or groups with purchasing power who are willing to exchange their resources for something else.

Markets can take different forms. This assumption implies there is a grouping of markets that are similar within, but different between. The alternative would be to believe that all markets are the same, which some economists assume, or that they are all different, which is what some marketing practitioners suggest. In economics, the main criteria by which one can distinguish between different market forms are the number and size of producers and consumers within the market, the type of goods and services being traded, and the degree to which information can flow freely. According to this categorization, there are seven major market forms[3]:

1. Perfect competition: The market consists of a very large number of firms producing products in the same domain.
2. Monopolistic competition: There is a large number of somewhat independent firms.
3. Oligopoly: A market is dominated by a small number of sellers.
4. Oligopson: A market dominated by many sellers and a few buyers.
5. Monopoly: There is only one provider of a product or service.
6. Natural monopoly: A monopoly in which economies of scale cause efficiency to increase continuously with the size of the firm.
7. Monopsony: There is only one buyer in a market.

Market forms are not fixed. The same market can change its form, e.g. from a prior monopoly to a current oligopoly or from a prior monopsony to a oligopsony. Mixed market forms tend to occur under various circumstances as well. The three analysed Philippine markets in this thesis have both many sellers and buyers. Correspondingly, their market forms approximate to the perfect competition.

2.1.2 Strategic Product Planning

Participants often have different intentions entering a market. Whereas buyers (e.g. private persons) are interested in purchasing products, sellers (e.g. private companies) want to maximise profit. An important aspect considering markets is the individual strategy, participants use to ensure their benefits. Therefore, this section gives an overview about market-oriented strategic (product) planning.

Kotler[4] defines strategic planning as follows: "The aim of strategic planning is to shape the company's businesses, products, services and messages so that they achieve targeted profits and growth" (quotation, p. 84). There are a number of tools that can be used in the area of strategic product planning, which common function is to lead entrepreneurs to profits. Very established ones among them are for instance the product life cycle, the Boston Consulting Group Growth-Share Matrix and the General Electric Market Attractiveness-Competitive Position Model. Another widespread tool is named Ansoff's Product-Market Expansion Grid, which will be explained below. A comprehensive overview of different strategic (product) planning approaches can be found in Jobber[5].

A useful way of looking at growth opportunities is the Ansoff Matrix, as shown in Figure 1. By combining existing and new products and existing and new markets into a 2 x 2 matrix, four product strategies for growth are revealed.

Figure 1: Ansoff's Product-Market Expansion Grid

Products

		Existing	New
	Existing	Market Penetration	Product Development
Markets	**New**	Market Development	Diversification

A company using the Ansoff Matrix is first to consider whether it could gain more market share with its current products in its current markets, e.g. by winning competitor's customers or increasing usage rates (market-penetration strategy). Next is to consider whether it can find or develop new markets for its current products, e.g. by entering new market segments or by promoting new uses of current products (market-development strategy). Then the company should consider whether it can develop new products of potential interest for its current markets, e.g. by product replacement or innovations (product-development strategy). Finally, opportunities to develop new products for new markets should be reviewed (diversification strategy).

This is the most risky option, especially when the entry strategy is not based on the company's core competences.

There are plenty of examples for all four growth strategies occurring in the Philippine markets. Mobile retailers penetrate the market by offering promotional sales in order to poach customers from their competitors. They also try to develop markets and appeal directly to children to buy their handsets. Retailers selling home appliances permanently innovate new products to extend their range of items and remain attractive. Audio visual retailers diversify their strategy and offer digital steel cameras to win new customers from associated markets.

2.2 Basic Principles of Retailing

This section introduces into the retail industry. Functions of retailing, various retail forms and aspects of the retail environment are presented. This overview is given to simplify the classification and understanding of the later expositions.

2.2.1 Definitions and Functions of Retailing

Retailing is all around us. It is as old as ancient trade routes and as new as the World Wide Web. Retailing is local, regional, national, international and global. As much of a country's wealth is accrued through some form of retailing, retail sales are a significant contributor to the Gross Domestic Product (GDP). Retailing is a significant part of business, placed under the big umbrella of marketing. Some authors like Hasty and Reardon[6] even compare retailing with marketing. Retailing is the most important link in the journey from producer to consumer. It is the selling of goods or services directly to the final customer for personal, non-business use. This definition implies that retail transactions involve rather small quantities of merchandise. Poloian[7] defines retailers as "businesses or individuals who sell more than 50 percent of their goods and or services to final customers" (quotation, p. 8). The total of all attempts retailers engage themselves in to satisfy their customers is called *retail mix*. Important aspects of it are merchandising, pricing, promoting and distributing. The merchandising or merchandise assortment consists of all the goods in a store, defined by their breadth and depth of stock. In contrast, according to Berman and Evans[8], *wholesaling* is an intermediate stage in the distribution process.

Instead of final consumers, goods and services are sold to business customers (such as manufacturers and retailers). Retailing is the last stage in a *channel of distribution* consisting of the physical movement and transfer of ownership of goods and services from producer to consumer. Retailers play a key role in the process. In a typical distribution channel, they are the contact point between manufacturers, wholesalers, other suppliers and the final consumer.

Poloian highlights six different functional areas of retailing. Since none of these can work isolated, they need to be coordinated permanently.

1. Merchandising: Includes all sourcing, buying and selling activities
2. Operations: All aspects of managing the physical plant, like warehousing
3. Promotion: Advertising, public relations and sales promotion events
4. Finance: Accounting, taxation and controlling the company's assets
5. Human Resources: Recruiting, training and evaluation of personnel
6. Information Technology: Technological support, crosses the first five areas

2.2.2 Classification Methods for Retail Institutions

The first classification method is *by ownership* (adopted from Berman and Evans, chapter four). Retail firms may be independently owned, chain-owned, franchisee-operated, leased departments, owned by manufacturers or wholesalers, or consumer-owned. Most retail estab-lishments are independent, each operating one store only. This high number of independent retailers is associated with the uncomplicated entry into the marketplace. However, due to the low number of shops of each retailer, extensive use of economies of scale cannot be realized. Chain-owned retailers are multiple stores under common ownership, usually with some centralized purchasing and decision-making. The entry barrier is higher than for independent retailers, because higher investments are necessary. Franchisee-operated retail institutions have a contractual arrangement between the franchisor (e.g. a manufacturer) and the franchisee, which allows the franchisee to conduct a given form of business under an estab-lished name and an existing business concept. The franchise principle is getting more and more popular among the retail industry, as it combines the benefit of a strong partner with elements of self-deployment. Leased departments are in-store locations, which are rented to outside parties. Normally, the proprietor of a leased department is responsible for all aspects of his business and pays a percentage of sales as rent. He may have to accept operating   restrictions. It is also possible that manufacturers own a retail institution, which is similar to independently owned businesses. Finally, consumer cooperatives are retail firms owned by their customer members, who invest, manage operations and share the profits.

A second classification approach is *by a store-based strategy mix*, which divides the retailers into food-oriented and general merchandise groupings. There are 14 store-based strategy mixes, from which five representative ones now will be explained. A convenience store is usually a well-located food-oriented retailer. Due to its small size, it carries just a moderate number of items. Prices are at least average (or above), and there is only moderate promotion. 7-Eleven is a US-convenience store. In opposition, a conventional supermarket is much bigger in size, usually departmentalized and carries a wide range of food and related items. Prices are competitive and there is heavy use of promotion. Albertson's is an example for a US-supermarket. Another type of food retailers is named Hypermarkets. The world's largest one is Carrefour from France. They offer the store-within-a-store concept (such as shoe repair shops, pharmacies and travel agencies) and create an innovative atmosphere with prices tendentiously lower than average. Hypermarkets are currently becoming popular in Asia. As they need a great population density (more than one million people within a 30-minute radius) to make their concept work, conditions seem to be fine there. The most common general merchandise store-based retailer is the traditional department store. It is a large retail unit with an extensive assortment of goods and services, organized into separate departments. Prices are average or above and frequent advertisements are published. Finally, speciality stores hold a different strategy. Opposite to a mass marketing approach, they concentrate on one goods or service line and use a tailored strategy. Speciality retailers have competitive prices and use many displays to promote their goods.

After the description of these retail classification methods, two special forms of retail institutions will be mentioned: Shopping Centres and Shopping Malls. Both of them are a lot more common in Asia than in Europe. A shopping centre is "a group of retail and other commercial establishments that is planned developed, owned and managed as a single property" (quotation from Poloian, p. 344). The difference to Shopping

Malls is the fact, that early shopping centres were not covered by a central roof. Poloian defines a mall as "a climate controlled structure in which retail stores are architecturally connected" (quotation, p. 345). Next to the basic types of shopping centres, several hybrid forms exist. Providing shopping experiences that satisfy several needs simultaneously is crucial to the success of newer formats. A current example is Megamalls, which are mainly built in North America and Asia. A Megamall is a mixed-use mall of well over one million square feet, accommodating 400 to 800 stores, service businesses and entertainment facilities.

The retail institutions examined in this dissertation are all classified as either independent or chain-owned (organized, see section 5.1). Talking about a store-based classification, there are, apart from several market specific shops, also traditional department stores and hypermarkets included. Many of them are located inside one of the country's numerous shopping centres and malls.

2.2.3 Retail Environment

The *retail environment* consists of a set of (un-)controllable variables[9]. Economic factors, like the interest rate, cyclical fluctuation or consumer's purchasing power influence the retail planning process. Higher retail sales can be expected in boom times than during recession. Changes in political regimes and events causing political instability (like September 11) affect retailing worldwide. Formation of new trade alliances and the enacting of new laws can also concern the retail structure, as the *Philippine Retail Liberalization Act in 2000* has demonstrated (see section 5.3). The social environment also affects the retail business. Complementally, retailers have contributed to the solution of social problems in many areas: They are involved in urban affairs, they permanently improve their goods and services and they create employment opportunities. Retailers need to follow demographic changes in household composition, age mix, population size, ethnic groups and family income statistics. Information on gender issues, educational and occupational trends are also necessary to notice. Environmental concerns affect the retail business as well. Ecologically safe products, the procurement and application of less poisonous materials as well as energy conservation are topics respected among retailers. Various ethical frameworks of different people need to be integrated. Unpredictable events such as natural disasters, deaths of celebrities and acts of terrorism also affect retail sales. One of the most important elements in the retail environment of the 21st century is technology. Due to new and emerging technologies, basic processes of retailing have been simplified and accelerated. Furthermore, conducting retail business always implies a competitive background. Participants are supposed to use store planning techniques and market share oriented growth-strategies to remain competitive. One of the reasons for increasing competition is the relative ease to enter and turn away from the markets. This makes retailing extremely dynamic. The consumer itself is also likely to change its habits and shopping patterns. The rise in the number of working women has increased male participation in shopping and the demand for longer opening hours. Finally, the structure of retailing must be mentioned, which has experienced major changes as well. The most significant is probably the growth of bigger chain stores, which has gained mostly at the expense of independent retailers.

The number of environmental influences listed above clearly indicates the dynamic and somewhat unpredictable circumstances that retailers have to face in their daily business. Chapter five emphasizes some characteristics of the Philippine retail trade, which also influence the industry.

For further information about marketing aspects (section 2.1), the books listed at bibliographical references four and five are recommended. For further reading about retailing (section 2.2), those specified at number seven and eight are suggested.

---

[1] See Geoff Easton, Market Forms and Market Models (Lancaster University Management School Working Paper, 2004/2005, http://www.lums.co.uk/publications), p. 1.

[2] See William G. Zikmund and Michael d'Amico, Effective Marketing. Creating and Keeping Customers, 2nd edition (Cincinnati: South-Western College Publishing Company, 1998), p. 8.

[3] Adopted from Wikipedia (http://en.wikipedia.org/wiki/Market_forms).

[4] See Philip Kotler, Swee H. Ang, Siew M. Leong and Chin T. Tan, Marketing Management, An Asian Perspective, 3rd edition (Singapore: Prentice Hall, 2003), chapter 4.

[5] See David Jobber, Principles and Practice of Marketing, 4th edition (Berkshire: McGraw-Hill, 2004), chapter 9.

[6] See Ron Hasty and James Reardon, Retail Management (USA: McGraw-Hill, 1997), p. 10.

[7] See Linda G. Poloian, Retailing Principles. A global Outlook (USA: Fairchild Publications, Inc., 2003), p. 8.

[8] See Barry Berman and Joel R. Evans, Retail Management. A Strategic Approach, 8th edition (New Jersey: Prentice Hall, 2001), p. 3.

[9] See Peter J. McGoldrick, Retail Marketing (Berkshire: McGraw-Hill, 1990), p. 63.

3. The Philippines

This chapter contains an introduction to the Philippines[10]. Besides facts and figures, a historical and socio-cultural[11] outline is presented. Finally, a brief description of the economical and political situation[12] of the country is given.

3.1 Facts and Figures

The Republic of the Philippines (Filipino: *Republika ng Pilipinas*), or the Philippines (Filipino: *Pilipinas*), also known as the Pearl of the Orient Seas, is an independent sovereign nation located in Southeast Asia. It lies 1,210 km away from mainland Asia and consists of 7,107 islands that form in physical geography a part of the Malay Archipelago. The total land area of the Philippines is about 300,000 km². The eleven largest islands contain 94% of it. The biggest of these islands is Luzon at about 105,000 km², followed by Mindanao at about 94,600 km². The total coastline is approx. 36,289 km. There is currently a total of 87,857,473 Filipinos (July 2005 estimated value). Population density is 276/km², which is ranked 27th worldwide. Population growth is approximately 1.84% annually. Luzon, the largest island group, accounts for more than half of the entire population. Almost 50% of the population is less than 20 years old, and about two thirds are less than 30 years old.

Under the constitution of 1987, the national language is Filipino, which is based on Tagalog. The official languages are Filipino and English, the latter being the medium of instruction in higher education. The Philippines is the third largest English speaking country in the world. Besides the official languages, there are eight major dialects spoken by a majority of the Filipinos: Tagalog, Cebuano, Ilocano, Hiligaynon, Bicol, Waray, Pampango, and Pangasinense. Almost 80% of Filipinos belong to the Roman Catholic religion, about 15% are Moslem. The rest consists of smaller Christian denominations and Buddhist.

3.2 Historical and Socio-Cultural Outlook

Portuguese and Spanish explorers, led by Ferdinand Magellan, first set foot on the archipelago in 1521. On 27 April 1565, Miguel López de Legazpi established the first permanent Spanish settlement on the island of Cebu (South of Philippines). The Philippines remained a Spanish colony until 1821. From 1821 to 1898, the Philippines was a Spanish province. Following the Spanish-American War in 1898, the country came under American occupation and became the first and only colony of the United States. In 1935, it became an unincorporated territory of the United States, in the form of a commonwealth. The Commonwealth Period was interrupted by World War II, when the Philippines came under Japanese occupation. During this time, they waged a guerrilla war against the Japanese from 1941 to 1945. The Philippines finally achieved de facto independence on 4 July 1946 (over 380 years after its first occupation).

The Philippines is one of the most ethnically diverse countries in Asia. Due to its past, the country has a rich history combining Asian, European (especially Spanish) and American influences and is marked by a true blend of cultures. In the Philippines, east meets west. The background of the people is primarily Indonesian and Malay, but there are Chinese and Spanish elements as well. Perhaps due to their long association with Spain, Filipinos are emotional and passionate about life in a way that seems more Latin than Asian. In terms of nationalistic organization, politics and government they also resemble these countries more closely. Furthermore, they are greatly directed towards Hispanic customs and traditions. All over Southeast Asia, they are especially well known for their hospitality.

The history of American rule and contact with merchants and traders has undoubtedly left its traces too, in both appearance and culture of the Filipinos. Being a predominantly Catholic nation, the Catholic Church has also had much influence on the people. However, due to modernization, the once very conservative Filipino has learned to be more liberated. Through the years, e.g. preferences in marrying age have greatly changed. For a Filipino male, just about 10-15 years ago, the age of 25 years old was a proper age to get married. Within the last 5 years, this has moved up to 32 to 35 years. Today, Filipino women hold high positions in society and many businesses. However, the tradition of strong family loyalty is still kept. Only the highland Negrito Filipinos, who live in the mountains of Luzon and Mindanao, have retained the ancient beliefs of their ancestors and isolate themselves from the modern day society. Their way of life is seen as the true indigenous culture of the Philippine archipelago.

3.3 Economical Situation

The Philippines was less severely affected by the Asian financial crisis of 1998 than its neighbours were. It was aided in part by annual remittances of USD 7 to 8 billion from overseas workers (see below) and no sustained run-up in asset prices or foreign borrowing prior to the crisis. From a 0.6% decline in 1998, GDP expanded by 2.4% in 1999 and by 4.4% in 2000. Because of a global economic slowdown, an export slump and unsafe political and security concerns, it slowed to 3.2% in 2001. GDP growth accelerated to 4.3% in 2002, 4.7% in 2003, and almost 6% in 2004. Compared to GDP rates from other Asian countries, these are still quite low. Total GDP was approx. USD 85 billion in 2004 (2005: USD 91.8 billion estimated). The GDP per capita was approx. USD 1,000. These results reflect the continued resilience of the service sector (53% of GDP), improved exports (industry: 32% of GDP) and agricultural output (15% of GDP).

In 2004, the value of exported goods summed up to USD 38.63 billion. Main export commodities have been electronic equipment, machinery and equipment, garments and coconut products. Next to the United States (17.5%), major export partners are Japan (15.8%) and China (11.4%). Germany has a share of 4.2%, the second largest one after the Netherlands in Europe. As the Philippines imports goods for USD 37.5 billion, the balance of trade is slightly positive. Most frequent import commodities have been raw materials, machinery and equipment, fuels and vehicles. Japan (20.6%) is the biggest trading partner ahead of USA (16%), Singapore (8.4%) and China (7.4%).

The current Filipino labour force is about 36 million with an unemployment rate of almost 12%. The percentage of the population living below the national poverty line is 40%. Like in other Southeast Asian countries, the distribution of wealth is very unbalanced: About 4% of the rich people possess 85% of the whole country's properties. It will take a higher, sustained growth path to make appreciable progress in poverty alleviation given the Philippines' high annual population growth rate and unequal distribution of income. The Philippines also faces higher oil prices, higher interest rates on its dollar borrowings, and higher inflation (which was 5.5% in 2004, and over 8% in the first half of 2005). Fiscal constraints limit the country's ability to finance infrastructure and social spending. The Philippines' consistently large budget deficit has produced a high debt level (public debts are about 80% of GDP). Therefore, Manila is forced to spend a large portion of the national budget on debt service only. Large, unprofitable public enterprises, especially in the energy sector, contribute to the government's debts because of slow progress on privatization. Prospects for the future depend heavily on the economic performance of the two major trading partners, the United States and Japan, and a more accountable administration and consistent government policies. The government will increasingly have to rely on foreign capital to meet its investment targets. To date, the Philippines has performed rather poorly compared with its neighbours in attracting inward investment. However, the country holds opportunities: Outsourcing could provide the Philippines, with its cheap English-speaking workforce, with a valuable source of foreign exchange.

There are only a few countries in the world, from which so many people leave their homes to work abroad than in the Philippines. The Filipino overseas community[13] (mostly in North America, Europe and the Middle East) is about 900,000 people strong and one of the biggest worldwide (see Figure 2). It will remain a key source of income for the country, as Overseas Filipino Workers (OFW) earn about USD 8 billion every year. This is equivalent to almost 10% of the GDP. As these US-Dollars can be brought into the country tax-free, there is an enormous number of remittances coming from OFW year by year, which stabilize the Philippine economy considerably.

Figure 2: Deployment and Remittances of Overseas Filipino Workers
(OFW), 2000-2003

OFW Deployment and Remittances, 2000–2003

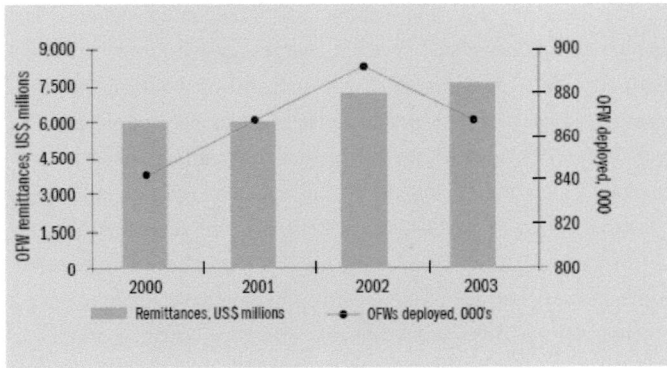

3.4 Political Outlook

The Philippines is a founding and active member of the United Nations since 24
October, 1945. It is also a founding and prominent member of the Association of
Southeast Asian Nations (ASEAN) and an active participant of the Asia-Pacific
Economic Cooperation (APEC). The government of the Philippines, loosely
patterned after the American system, is organized as a representative republic, with
the President functioning as both head of state and government, as well as being the
commander-in-chief of the armed forces. The president is elected by popular vote to a
term of six years, during which he or she appoints and presides over the cabinet. The
bicameral Philippine legislature, the congress, consists of the senate and the house of
representatives. Members of both are elected by popular vote. There are 24 senators
serving six years in the senate while the house of representatives consists of no more
than 250 congressmen each serving three-year terms. The judiciary branch of the
government is headed by the supreme court, which has a chief justice as its head and
14 associate justices, all appointed by the president.

The current president (since January 20, 2001), who was elected in May 2004 for six more years, is named Gloria Macapagal-Arroyo. The vice president is called Manuel De Castro. They govern Asia's oldest democratic unitary republic. The Philippines is a vibrant democracy according to twelve English national newspapers, seven national television stations, hundreds of cable TV stations and 2,000 radio stations. The government is pursuing corruption-related criminal charges against former president Estrada, who is currently under detention. The not insignificant political influence from diverse business tycoons or celebrities has also tried to be diminished. The terrorist Abu Sayyaf Group (ASG), which recently gained international notoriety with bombings and kidnappings of foreign tourists in the southern islands, is a major problem for the government. In May 2001, the ASG kidnapped several Americans that it still holds. Efforts to track down and destroy the ASG have been unsuccessful. Banditry, rising crime and concerns about the security situation have begun to have a negative impact on tourism and foreign investment. The government continues to face threats from both Muslim separatist groups and communist insurgents and is pursuing peace talks with both groups.

---

[10] For further reading, see Wikipedia (http://de.wikipedia.org/wiki/Philippinen).

[11] Information adopted from CIA Factboo
(http://www.cia.gov/cia/publications/factbook/geos/rp.html#Intro).

[12] Information adopted from Philippine Business
(http://www.philippinebusiness.com.ph/guide/prc00.htm).

[13] Information taken from GfK Asia E-News Letter, Philippine Edition, January 2005, Vol. 1, p. 11.

4. The GfK Group

This chapter reports about the GfK Group. First, a general overview about the company's activities is given[14]. Then, the most elaborate business unit and the *GfK Methodology* are explained. Finally, the chapter reveals information about GfK Asia and the subsidiary in the Philippines.

4.1 Facts and Figures

In times of globalization, there is a growing demand for information about the global markets. GfK identified this trend at an early stage and started designing information systems with an international and global focus. Nowadays, GfK offers uniform information that takes account of national and regional differences. The company's aim is to provide clients from industry, retail, media and the service sector with information services that can be applied in the most varied ways to support their activities. The GfK Group is a German company, established in 1934. It is the country's largest market research organization and the number four worldwide. GfK stands for *Growth from Knowledge*. It has over 130 subsidiaries and affiliates (21 of them in Germany) located in 63 countries. Of a current total of more than 7,000 employees, approximately 1,500 are based at the headquarters in Nuremberg, Germany. The GfK Group had total sales of EUR 672 million for the financial year 2004, with a profit of EUR 64 million. The estimated turnover for the year 2005 is EUR 911 million, with a profit of EUR 75 million.

On June 1, 2005, GfK acquired the market research group NOP World from the British United Business Media for a sum of approx. 550 million Euro. With over 1,500 NOP employees joining GfK, the Group has considerably expanded its team. NOP World and the GfK Group recorded joint sales of almost one billion Euro in 2004. The GfK Group is likely to become number three in the world this year, as the distance in turnover to the actual third of the sector, the British Kantar Group, has become very small.

According to turnover, Germany is still the most important single market for the GfK Group (see Figure 3): It accounted for 37% of total sales in 2003. The second region with a sales volume of more than EUR 200 million is Western and Southern Europe (35%). Total Europe accounted for almost 50% of sales. America and Asia both had a comparably small share (8% and 6%, respectively).

Figure 3: Share of regions in total sales of 2003

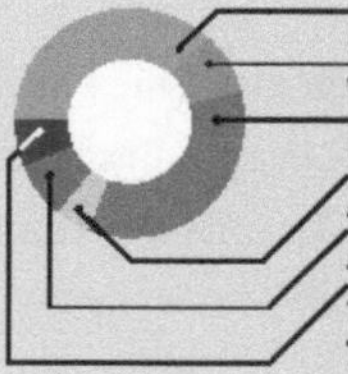

Share of regions in total sales 2003[1]	in %	in EUR million
Germany	37	221.7
Northern Europe	9	54.1
Western and Southern Europe	35	204.7
Central and Eastern Europe	5	31.8
America	8	48.6
Asia and the Pacific	6	34.3
Total	100	595.3

1) Rounding differences may occur

4.2 GfK's Five Business Divisions

GfK's services are organized into five business divisions:

- Custom Research: Information services for developing, positioning and maintaining products and services, aimed at optimizing the mix of marketing policy activities and managing product and corporate brands and customer loyalty.

- Retail and Technology: Information services regarding marketing, sales, logistics in retail and industry for companies operating in consumer technology markets. Includes the continuous and systematic observation of sales trends in consumer durables.

- Consumer Tracking: Information services regarding market and marketing matters relating to day-to-day consumer buying decisions and habits, providing information on almost all fast moving consumer goods plus a large number of slow moving consumer goods and services.

- Health Care: Information services relating to product development, communication, image and price control of medicines, market positioning and customer satisfaction, measuring the unit number and sales of materials and products used by dentists and laboratories, as well as measuring the consumption of veterinary medicines.

- Media: Information services on media consumer behaviour and attitudes. Services include quantitative analyses of viewer, reader and listener reach and qualitative surveys on acceptance, preferences and recall of media content. The most known is the "GfK Fernsehforschung" that carries out continuous electronic measurement of German TV audience.

4.3 Retail and Technology

This section offers a more detailed view of the Retail and Technology division[15], because the research done in this thesis belongs to that segment. Retail and Technology is the most elaborate business unit of the GfK Group. It monitors consumer technology, particularly IT, telecommunications, electronic entertainment, household electrical appliances, photographic equipment and do-it-yourself products. Generally, GfK only tracks the sales of goods from retailers to consumers, not from wholesalers to consumers or direct sales from manufacturers. The GfK *coverage rate* (percentage, to which all sales of a certain market are covered) of the total market is usually about 80% to 85%. Retail and Technology mainly provides information about sales, purchases, stocks and distribution of individual items. The range of data provided facilitates a comprehensive analysis from the smallest unit, the model, via the brand to the market as a whole. These data allow decision-makers to analyze their product structure, pricing and distribution policy and their position in relation to the competition. The analysis of a company's positioning, as well as that of competitors also provides a picture of its own strengths, weaknesses, opportunities and threats.

Retail and Technology business information services are based on *retail panels* covering all the key types of outlets in the sectors concerned. Retail panels (also called *retail audit*) are regular surveys that monitor sales of particular products and categories of products in a sample of various types of retail outlets. In other words, they are representative samples for defined outlets, delivering measured facts about sales, purchases, stocks, selling prices and distribution of individual items. Most of the information is obtained by electronic data interchange between GfK and these retailers. GfK's worldwide master file database contains over 450,000 individual items in over 100 sectors. In Europe, Asia and the USA, GfK is the world's leading retail tracking services provider for electrical household appliances, electronic entertainment and telecommunications.

Retail panels supply the required data at regular intervals. The data are then compiled and translated into useful information using statistically proven methods. GfK's services include monthly, weekly and even daily information about market structures and developments (e.g. size of market by value and volume, market structures according to sales channel or the market share by brand and model). For decision-makers, these data form the basis for research and development, production planning, control of distribution and marketing. GfK covers three of the four P's known in the marketing literature as the *Marketing Mix*: Product, Price and Place. The remaining one, Promotion, can be deduced out of these three.

Usually, those retailers joining the GfK panel and contributing to the GfK data pool receive (part of) their relevant market information free of charge in return. GfK regularly publishes detailed reports about certain products, brands and markets in different countries, which are sold to the corresponding Original Equipment Manufacturers (OEM). GfK offers both country specific reports on certain regions and economic areas as well as client specific reports.

4.4 GfK Methodology

This section provides a description of the GfK Methodology[16]. Principally, GfK collects data from retailers, analyses and finally sells them to manufacturers in the form of reports. To collect the data, GfK dispatches data sheets to all retailers in the panel, both manually and electronically. The retailers fill in these sheets and GfK gathers them. After controlling the data, they are submitted to a central department responsible for the final data checking (of a certain region). After that, they can be presented to clients and the reports can be written.

The total of all existing retailers of a certain market in a certain country defines the *retailer universe*. To determine its number, every retail shop of this market needs to be counted. This process is called the *universe count*. As it is impossible to collect data from every retailer, GfK always tries to get a *representative sample* of the universe. The sample building process follows a fixed procedure. To obtain a sample representative for the whole market, approximately 10% to 20% of all existing retailers need to be included. The random selection of the shops follows a calculated quota, by which different shop types, sizes and distribution channels are taken into account. The ratio between universe and sample is called *factor* (Universe / Sample = Factor). If the universe count results in a universe of 1,000 retail shops and the sample consists of one hundred, the factor is 1,000 / 100 = 10. As 10 is an appropriate factor size, the sample can be considered as representative for the universe.

The aforementioned is only valid for *independent shops* (see section 5.1). For *organized shops*, the factor is always one by definition. That implies GfK has to cover all organized shops in the universe, because every one of them needs to be included in the sample. This is because organized shops are very likely to be too different from each other, which makes them unsuitable for data projection purposes (see below). Consequently, the selected sample is usually *disproportional*, meaning that its relative number of organized shops (from the universe) is higher than those of its independent shops. To maximise the representative constitution of a sample, shops with bigger market shares should more frequently be included than those with smaller. This practice further increases the disproportional structure of the sample.

GfK

Once the usage of the GfK *sampling method* has led to a representative sample, its data are analysed. The results are finally projected to the whole universe by *linear extrapolation*. This process is called *data projection*. It enables GfK to make conclusions and generalizations valid for the whole market, though derived only from a sample. The principle is illustrated in a short example: If a universe consists of 500 shops and a derived sample of 50, the factor is 10. Assuming these 50 shops sell 1,000 units of a certain product X (model Y, brand Z) per day, the projection to the total market size (defined by the total of units sold) results in 1,000 x 10 = 10,000 units. To obtain the number of units sold in the universe, the number of units sold in the sample has to be multiplied by the factor.

In summary, the GfK Methodology can be depicted as a *Matrix Management*, which is illustrated in Figure 4. A matrix is a numerical frame of data based on a number of cells reflecting the total number of shops in the universe per distribution channel (1, 2, 3), per region (A, B, C), and per shop size measured in turnover (Small, Medium, Large). The matrix is product category based (e.g. white goods). According to the left part of the matrix, there are for instance 120 shops in the universe, which correspond to channel 1, region A and turnover size S. The middle part of the figure shows the representative sample that has been derived from the universe. 10 shops with channel 1, from region A and with turnover size S have been randomly chosen. The right part of Figure 4 illustrates the projection of the sample results to the universe by linear extrapolation. Thus, reliable estimations of the "true" parameters of the universe can be obtained.

Figure 4: The GfK Methodology depicted as a Matrix Management

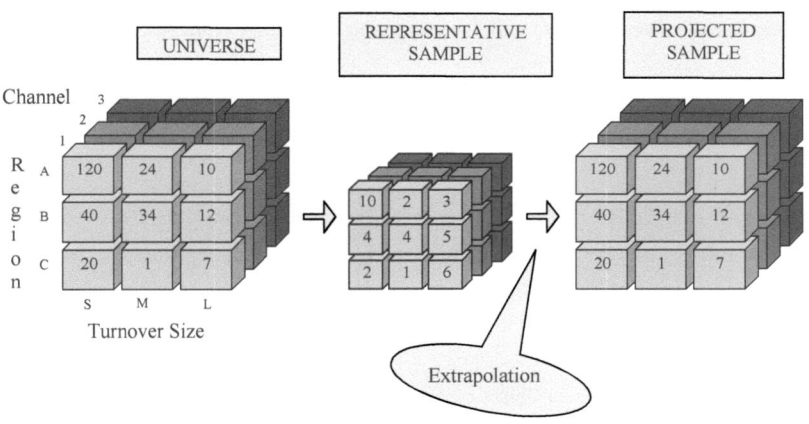

4.5 GfK Asia

The History of GfK Asia[17] started 20 years ago (1985) in Japan. Nowadays, the Asia and Pacific region is comprised of 17 GfK subsidiaries in 14 countries: Australia, Cambodia, China, Hong Kong, Indonesia, Japan, New Zealand, Malaysia, Philippines, Singapore, South Korea, Taiwan, Thailand and Vietnam. The latest branches have been opened in Cambodia and the Philippines (both 2004). The Head Office of GfK Asia is in Singapore, responsible for the distribution and sales of the reports to manufacturers all over the continent. GfK Asia only operates in the Retail and Technology division.

There are nearly 500 full-time employees working for GfK Asia. At almost 25%, the companies in these countries achieved the highest organic growth of any region covered by GfK branches. This reflects the efforts of the GfK Management to speed-up the business in Asia. In an interview with the German business magazine Focus-Money[18] in July of 2005, the CEO Dr. Klaus Wübbenhorst stated that GfK Asia strives to increase its sales up to EUR 100 million in the next years. In 2004, turnover was approx. 40 million Euro. The profit margin has been 17.6%. The GfK Group is especially expanding its HealthCare research activities. The latest acquisition from August 1, 2005 is the market research specialist SoHealthAsia in Hong Kong. This move is one of the first strategic steps towards expanding the HealthCare network into the principle Asian markets with the establishment of GfK branches.

4.6 GfK Philippines

Since September 2004, the GfK Group has opened a new subsidiary in the Philippines. It is located right in the business district of Manila. Under the lead of their General Manager, Mr. Vu the Du from Vietnam, the nine employees generated an estimated turnover of approx. USD 100.000 in 2004.

Since the Philippines has been fairly isolated, and as foreign investors only recently started to be interested in the archipelago (see section 5.3), it was not possible to enter the huge country with its consume-oriented inhabitants any earlier. Generally, it is more promising for GfK to engage in markets with plenty of foreign investors (like Thailand), because these foreign investors often demand the GfK reports about the local retail structure. This puts some pressure on the local retailers to join the GfK panel, which brings GfK into a comfortable position. This is still different for the Philippines; extensive recruitment activities are necessary to win clients there.

GfK Philippines currently tracks eight products from three different product categories.

1. Audio Visuals (AV)
- Audio Home Systems
- Camcorders
- Colour TVs
- Visual Displayers (DVD, VCD)

2. Home Appliances (HA)

- Air-Conditioning
- Refrigerators
- Washing Machines

3. Mobile phones

- Mobile Handsets

---

[14] For further reading, see the GfK Homepage (http://www.gfk.com).

[15] Information adopted from "GfK Non-Food Tracking" Brochure (2003).

[16] Information taken from "GfK Asia Retail Service Version" (August 2004).

[17] Information taken from "GfK Asia Corporate Presentation" (August 2004).

[18] Andreas Hanslauer, GfK: Champions League (Focus Money, 20th of July 2005), p. 16-17.

5. Local Characteristics of the Philippine Retail Structure

This section presents some local characteristics [19] of the retail structure in the Philippines. In addition to that, it reports about the enactment of the *retail trade liberalization law* in the year 2000. As GfK permanently has to cope with the local circumstances, the last section discusses problems and implications for the company.

5.1 Independent and Organized Retailers

In terms of GfK, the Philippine retail trade consists of two different types of shops, named independent and organized. As indicated by the name, independent shops are autonomous and not dependent from other shops. They are often run by families, which only own one shop. Since there are no corporate identity regulations for independent shops, their equipment and design can vary considerably, especially between different markets (e.g. the mobile market and the electronic goods market). Within the same market, independent shops usually look quite similar to even interchangeable.

On the other side, GfK considers a cluster of several shops that belong together as organized. Whereas every independent shop usually belongs to another owner, several organized shops are owned by the same person. They are often run by families and follow the same corporate design regulations, which make them easier to recognise. Their equipment, design and offered product range is always standardized. All shops have the same name, too. Organized shops are comparable to chain stores. Beside other locations, independent and organized shops are frequently found in many of the numerous shopping centres and malls in Manila.

5.2 Typical Filipino Retailers

The typical Filipino retailer is different from the German one. Especially independent retail shops can be very small, sometimes only about two to five square meters. This primarily results from the relatively high rental fees that can go up to over 30,000

Philippine Pesos ($\approx$ 438 Euro[20]) a month for five square meters, depending on the quality of the location. Most independent shops are equipped very basically. The interior decoration often consists of small tables, on which the goods and further accessories are placed. The available space is completely used, meaning that there is very little space between the items. This gives the impression that every shop is somewhat crowded and it is difficult to overlook the merchandise. Since there is normally no space between the neighbouring shops, they seem to be indistinguishable, comparable to German flea markets. It can therefore be quite hard to determine to which shop a particular item belongs. These circumstances and the fact there might be dozens of shops in a row, give the impression that all of them seem to offer the same things. Organized shops usually look more European, as they are bigger, cleaner and well-ordered. For the more sophisticated and prestige oriented customer with sufficient purchase power, they are nowadays the place to go in the Philippines.

Compared to western countries, the number of retailers is considerably higher in the Philippines. This results from the Filipino "foundation culture". For the national people, running an own business is more respectable than being employed. Their motivation is not only profit, as Filipinos are not known to be greedy and the average margins are not extraordinary high. Nonetheless, many of them try to open a shop, selling whatever goods they are able to get. It seems their lifestyle is distinctively directed towards self-employment in the retailing business. Correspondingly, locals own far more shops than foreign investors.

Since the typical retailer is very conservative and there are very close family ties among the competitors, it is common that the management involves the entire family. Most of the retailers in the country are either Filipino or Chinese business people. Many Filipinos are related to Chinese people, whose local chain stores dominate the market. There are about 5% pure Chinese people in the Philippines, and about 15% Filipino-Chinese, that had been born and educated there.

5.3 The Retail Liberalization Law

The major businesses in the Philippines were developed about 60 years ago, directly after World War II, under the strong participation of the government. Since then, the governmental institutions and the business conditions have not really changed. Persons in charge still practice old business formulas and are said to be adherent to traditional commerce and secrecy. Until recently, the Philippines has hardly opened the door to its neighbouring or western countries. International interested parties have not been allowed to make noticeable investments in the country. The Southeast Asian archipelago figuratively speaking cut itself off from the rest of the world.

However, things have changed. The country's peak of isolation belongs to the past. Economically speaking, circumstances are slowly getting better for the Philippines. A basic prerequisite enabling this change was the enactment of the retail trade liberalization law[21] on March 26, 2000. By releasing this important law in the framework of the retail trade liberalization act of 2000, the government gave its allowance for foreigners to invest in the Philippine industries. Foreign ownership of Philippine retail enterprises depends on the amount of the enterprise's capitalization. Retail ventures with paid-up capital less than the Philippine Peso equivalent of USD 2,500,000 (Category A) is limited to Filipinos. Initially, within two years after the act became effective (until March 26, 2002), foreign investors could only own up to 60% of retail enterprises with paid-up capital between USD 250 million and USD 750 million (Category B). Full foreign ownership of such ventures was permitted after this two-year period. Enterprises that have paid-up capital greater than USD 750 million (Category C), as well as those engaged in the retail of high-end or luxury items (Category D) are fully open to foreign investors.

Foreign entity willing to engage in the retail business or to invest in a Philippine retail store must meet various criteria. First, depending on the category, the parent corporation must have a certain net worth. Second, at least five retail stores or franchises anywhere in the world, or at least one branch with capitalization of USD 25 million or more need to be owned. Third, foreign retailers are prohibited from engaging in trade outside their accredited stores.

The Retail Trade Liberalization bill had several specific objectives[22]. It should empower 87 million Filipino consumers through more competition among retailers that will bring retail prices down, widen the range of choices and improve the quality of goods and services. It should help to promote the Philippines as a shopping Mecca in the Asia-Pacific region by completing the range of available goods and services that will attract a larger flow of tourist traffic into the country. It was supposed to provide local manufacturers with more windows to world markets through foreign retailers. Finally, it should improve employment terms for labour in the retail trade sector and expand employment opportunities in the manufacturing sector.

Five and a half years after the law came into force, some of these objectives have been reached. Foreign direct investments in the Philippines have increased substantially. Numerous international companies entered the low developed market. Facing a growing competition, local companies have been exposed to more pressure and started to go global, too. SM Mega Mall[23] is currently planning to open a shop in China, and other retailers follow the trend to go abroad in Asia. The consumer is the winner of these developments, sine local as well as international manufacturers have to improve the quality of their products and lower their selling prices to remain competitive.

5.4 Problems and Implications for GfK Philippines

Besides the advantages mentioned for the consumers, the multitude of local shop owners implicates some problems, too. Since there are far less restrictions and controlling instances concerning the opening and operation of a retail store in the Philippines, there are no established market structures yet that could be compared with western countries. The ongoing trade is still hard to overlook. Many retail shops are not registered and are run illegally. One of the main reasons for this is tax evasion. To keep their shops untraceable, owners frequently change their names and move regularly. A large amount of unauthorised retailers coexists next to the registered ones.

These circumstances have diverse implications for GfK Philippines. As described in the previous chapter, the task of GfK Philippines is to audit the retail trade in the country. For this purpose, a representative number of retailers need to join the GfK panel to enable the company to track the product sales. First, the concept of retail auditing has been relatively unknown in the Philippines, as GfK is the first company willing to measure the country's market activities systematically. Next to the point that retail auditing is not common in the Philippines, there is the thoughtless attitude of many local business people. Most of them are not interested in abstract, market-oriented figures like their sales volume of product X or the market share of competitor Y. They just want to make profit and thus believe these considerations are not of any importance to their daily management. Another reason for the resistance of many retailers lies in the nature of the information GfK is asking for. Even those generally willing to collaborate hesitate, because of the highly sensitive information they need to disclose. Afraid of being accused or reported to the police, they often refuse to work with GfK, especially if they run their shops illegally. It even happened that employees from GfK were thought to come from the government's department of tax evasion and asked to leave immediately. In order to reduce the retailer's uncertainty, GfK started to replace the expression "retail audit" with open circumscriptions like "retail survey" or "retail question-ing".

The attitude of shop owners managing bigger stores is usually somewhat less resistant. This might be attributed to their franker style of leadership and their stronger desire to build up efficient business networks. Many of them have been educated overseas.

Another problem for the retail audit is the instability of some markets (see section 7.3.2). Shops disappear over night or are not recognizable any more due to names or locations changed. As a result, the universe of shops is not constant. This has two implications for GfK: First, an accurate universe count is compounded. Second, there are many dropouts to record. However, a mutually satisfying business relationship between GfK and a retailer requires an uninterrupted provision of the necessary data. The consequences of inaccurate universe count estimations are far-reaching, even if they can partially be attenuated by statistical artefacts. Imprecisely adjusted sampling sizes may cause biased projections, which lead to incorrect forecasts about market figures. These finally deteriorate the quality of the GfK reports. A high dropout quota needs to be equalized through increased recruitment activities, which are time-consuming and expensive.

GfK Philippines certainly started to draw the necessary consequences from the current situation of the local retail market. In order to keep the data accurate, regular universe count estimations are carried out. According to the results, sample sizes and coverage rates are adjusted. In other words, the Philippine Matrices (see chapters seven to nine) are updated as frequently as possible. Unexpected dropouts are compensated by a higher number of retailers in the GfK panels as necessary for projection purposes.

---

[19] Information taken from „GfK Retail Service Presentation" (February 2005).

[20] 1 Euro ~ 68.55097 Philippine Pesos, valid August 24, 2005
(http://www.oanda.com/convert/classic).

[21] For further reading, see Department of Trade & Industry
(http://www.dti.gov.ph/contentment/9/63/281.jsp).

[22] Information taken from Philippine Embassy
(http://www.philembassy.au.com/download/nvestop_retail.pdf).

[23] See The Manila Times, March 29, 2005: Construction of P500-M SM-Clark starts
(http://www.manilatimes.net/national/2005/mar/29/yehey/prov/20050329pro5.html).

6. Interviews with Philippine Retailers

This part of the thesis contains the results of a series of interviews that have been conducted with nine Philippine Retailers. The goal of the survey was to take a closer look at the situation and perspective of these kinds of business people, which is important since GfK's core business depends on them. Although the number of questioned retailers is not representative for the universe of Philippine retailers, the results allow gaining some insight. The findings can at least be used for the development of working hypothesis that can be examined in further research.

6.1 Contents and Circumstances

Nine shop owners have been questioned about various topics, among them:

- their best-selling products
- their customers' needs and demands
- the influence of the Chinese market
- their relationship with their suppliers
- the mutual competition between independent and organized retailers.

The complete interview guide is included in appendix A. All interviews were conducted semi-structured and open. This technique implies on the one hand that the interviewer uses an interview guide, but the order of the questions posed is variable. On the other hand, no closed but only open questions have been asked. This method was chosen to preserve flexibility during the process of interviewing and to collect a maximum of information. To keep the retailers' time involved as low as possible, most interviews were conducted during recruitment activities or planned meetings between them and GfK staff. Each interview took about 20 minutes. The interviewer posed the questions and made a note of the answers.

The circumstances of the interviews have been very challenging. The whole procedure had to be completed quickly, since the shop owners were normally pressed for time. They often manage their store alone or are indispensable within the opening hours, so there was no possibility to change the location for the time of the interview. Therefore, the questioning usually took place in the middle of the store, between employees, customers and sometimes even suppliers. It also happened there was no place to sit, so that both interviewer and interviewee needed to stand with very little space. As the shop owner generally participates in all operations concerning his business and is often asked for advice, the interviews had to be interrupted frequently. Depending on the location of a shop, its noise level can be extremely high, especially for independent stores inside shopping malls. There are dozens of them right next to each other, normally without any dividing doors or soundproofing. One interview had to be completed with both interviewer and interviewee almost shouting at each other in order to understand what the opposite was saying.

Last, but not least, Manila is not a place visited by European people all too often. The locals, especially in poorer regions of the capital are not used to seeing foreigners in public shopping malls or industrial areas. The presence of a tall, white foreigner carrying out interviews with Filipinos seemed to have quite an entertainment value for some of them. It was common that Filipinos, especially children, "joined" the interview by rallying round the interviewer and his partner, staring and listening curiously to what was happening. Some of them were asking questions, others were giving answers to the questions actually posed to the interviewee.

Due to these challenging circumstances, the realization of the survey has been a unique and amusing experience for the interviewer. Appendix B contains a larger choice of the given answers to most questions. The following section contains a summary of these results.

6.2 Summary of Results

Nine interviews were conducted, five of them with mobile retailers, one with a white goods retailer and three with dealers of electrical appliances. The number of the owner's shops varied between 1 and 26 with an average of six stores per owner. About half of them were located in the business area of Manila (called *Metro Manila*), the others outside.

As most of the questioned retailers either had been satisfied or were at least not complaining about their sales in 2004, it seemed to be a good business year for them. For the mobile market, the best-selling products were Nokia models (mainly from the 3000 or 7000 series). Otherwise, DVD players and colour TVs were named. Besides generally cheap items, these products were also the ones customers asked for most regularly. Concerning customers' needs, the retailers definitely know how to satisfy their clients. Nevertheless, it happened that customers asked products knowing neither the price they are not willing to pay nor the features they could not do without. Further problems arose when customers com-plained about technical malfunctions of their goods that could not be repaired by the shop owner.

Almost all shop owners agreed that the influence of the Chinese market is noticeable. Many products traded in the Philippines are nowadays produced in China, especially cell phones. The Chinese market has become very strong over the past years, as Chinese brands are normally cheaper. However, the retailers did not agree about the quality of the Chinese products. Some meant it is roughly equivalent to the original brands, others said it is generally worse and products with comparable high quality are more expensive. They also gave heterogeneous statements concerning the question, if clients still prefer the pricier originals to the cheaper Chinese products. Some share the opinion this is still true and they normally do not tell their clients about the country of origin. Others agree that people bought goods dependent only on price.

The next question was aimed at the relationship between retailers and suppliers. Most shop owners saw this relationship as rather difficult and business related. There were always discussions about the purchase prices of goods. Some retailers had the impression that their suppliers do not care if they make profit or losses. They also criticised a decreased service level and the low stock available at many suppliers. Retailers had very similar expectations of their suppliers: First, they wait for low prices. Second, they expect the supplier to deliver good quality items. Third, they want good service and punctual delivery. Fourth, suppliers should take responsibility for faulty deliveries. Finally, they expect them to offer enough new products to ensure their customers have a great choice.

The last question asked was about the mutual competition between independent and organized retailers. Almost none of the independent shop owners feared the influence of organized shops. They shared the opinion that the market is big enough for both and enough customers favour the lower prices from independent retailers. The opposite opinion feared the organized shops because of their higher number of branches, stock volumes, and the possibility to pay with credit card (convenience shopping). The interviewed organized shop owners did not fear the influence of their independent counterparts. They rely on their bigger shop sizes, their better choice and their longer product guarantees. One retailer mentioned that both shop types were helping each other.

7. The Mobile Market in the Philippines

Chapter seven evaluates the Philippine mobile market. After a general description[24], the Philippine Matrices (see chapter 1) will be presented. The last section contains the market analysis and depicts a positioning matrix for the mobile market.

7.1 Description of the Philippine Mobile Market

Nowadays, the handset market can undoubtedly be considered as one of the hottest markets in the country. No other market is as fast developing and rapidly changing as the cell phone market, ranging from basic models suitable to make phone calls to smart phone versions with many additional functions that go far beyond the original purpose of a phone.

7.1.1 Market Overview: Current Competitors

The variety of mobile handsets in the Philippines is impressive. Subscribers have an almost endless range of different brands and models to choose from. As the market is very brand conscious, Chinese or local brands are not widespread. The Philippine mobile market is occu-pied by international manufacturers. Nokia, the current market leader, is willing to release 39 new models within the year 2005. Nokia is followed by an unclear second in the pack of SonyEricsson, Samsung and Motorola. Although Nokia tries to consolidate its lead, the mar-ket challengers are not far behind and competition is extraordinarily tough. Motorola, especially, has high ambitions to dethrone the current market leader in the next few years[25]. Samsung accomplished a major milestone in the company's history and changed the position-ing of its products from the low-end, through the mid-level, to high-end category. Crowned with success, Samsung seems to continue with this business strategy. Not all multinational companies are successful with their mobile business. One of the former stars, the German company Siemens, has recently sold its mobile division to the Chinese company BenQ. Siemens mobiles' poor performance is assumed to be due to the company's character of relea-seing new models in a rather late fashion compared with competitors. With all these multina-tional companies being engaged in the ongoing power struggle for the supremacy of the Philippine mobile market, it is realistic to predict that this market will remain one of the hottest in the future.

The mobile handset market is still a price driven low-end market. Most units sold are low-end products. Table 1 shows the hitlist of the top ten mobile sales in Manila of January 2005[26]. All prices have been converted into Euro. Almost all models belong to the low-end category with average prices between 50 to 100 Euro per unit. The only exception is the SonyEricsson K500I, which costs about 150 Euro. With more than 46,000 units sold, Nokia is the absolute predominant brand, serving the demand by successfully offering several low entry-level phones. SonyEricsson and Motorola share a comparable number of approximately 11,000 and 9,000 units, respectively. The fact Samsung does not appear in this hitlist can be attributed to its strategic repositioning from lower- to upper-class models, as previously mentioned.

Table 1: Hitlist of the top ten mobile sales in Manila (January 2005)

Rank	Model	Average Price (in Euro)	Quantities Sold
1	Nokia 1100	51	18.629
2	Nokia 3315	45	9.176
3	MOT C651	84	8.893
4	Nokia 6600	90	6.066
5	Nokia 3200	108	5.032
6	SonyEricsson T230	68	4.741
7	Nokia 2600	65	3.987
8	Nokia 2300	68	3.384
9	SonyEricsson K500I	153	3.369
10	SonyEricsson T610	112	3.009

7.1.2 Facts, Figures and Characteristics

The market penetration for mobile phones in the Philippines reached 35% in 2004 for the entire country[27]. There is a huge difference between the penetration rate in the capital and the rural provinces. The penetration rate for Manila is about 75%-80%, whereas it declines to 25% for the provinces. With a population of over 87 million, the Philippines currently has approx. 30 million mobile owners. Various estimates for 2005 show a market penetration of up to 50%, which would mean over 40 million users.

The Philippines is a "message-crazy" country[28]. About 10% of the worldwide number of daily messages sent stem from the Southeast Asian archipelago. The average mobile user sends 30 messages a day. Each domestic message costs one Philippine Peso (approx. 1.46 Eurocent). As there are about 30 million current subscribers in the

Philippines, the quantity of messages sent per day almost amounts to one billion. This gigantic magnitude is higher than for any other country in the world with a comparable number of subscribers.

Unlike the Short Message Services, the Multi Media Services are rarely used. Despite the fact that most new cell phones are MMS capable and the technology is available, subscribers do not fall back on it. This is mostly attributed to the higher expenditures for Multi Media Services than to missing appreciation for the technological progress. From simple SMS, the market is more than ever into downloading and sending ring tones, movie reservations or chatting. Another important add-on is the digital camera, which - just like polyphone ring tones - has become a minimum feature of modern mobile handsets.

It is less about the usage of these additional technological features than about the increased image factor they give rise to[29]. In the Philippines, the mobile telephone is not only considered as a tool that enables someone to make phone calls. On the contrary, the possession of especially high-end phones embodies wealth and creates the impression of being part of the high society. Modern cellular phones are sources of personal entertainment enriched with aspects of social status, which makes them suitable to support the "sunny side" of someone's personality. Apparently, all big mobile manufacturers are already aware of that: The number of *smart phones* (highly technological cell phones with a lot of additional features, e.g. integrated organizer functions) has increased considerably.

There are three big Network Service Providers[30] operating in the Philippines at present, named Globe Telecom, SMART Wireless and SUN Cellular. Years ago, people preferred to acquire their handsets from these three providers. Nowadays, a significant amount of revenue comes from independent shops or so called mobile kiosks, which are widely spread over the country and particularly concentrated in Manila. There are reasons for that phenomenon. Independent shops are generally cheaper than original providers are. Even more deciding is the fact that kiosks have an offering providers do not: They allow handset trade-ins. They are the only place where people can sell old units at a depreciated value and purchase a new handset on the spot with its selling price reduced by the value of the old phone. This avenue for trade-ins is probably the prime catalyst for a huge Philippine replacement market.

The replacement market could also be a good reason why Nokia is still the undisputed market leader. It is common for Filipinos to change their handsets quite often, sometimes every three months or whenever a new model is released. Many people buy Nokia models only because both their resale probability and value is higher than for any other currently existing brand. Part of their buying incentive merely results from the convenient replacement option.

People using the replacement market are not the only target group worth considering. The following chart (Table 2) contains four target groups, into which the market can be divided. They result from the combination of old versus new phones and old versus new SIM-cards.

Table 2: Four possible target groups in the mobile market

	Old Phone	**New Phone**
Old SIM-Card	Current Subscribers	Replacement Market
New SIM-Card	Subscriber Churn Rate (Switcher)	New Subscribers

The replacement market consists of people, who already possess old SIM-cards and now want to change their handsets. The new subscriber is a person, who has neither a phone nor a SIM-card. People with old phones who want to change their SIM-cards are called switchers. The number of switchers indicates the subscriber churn rate. The current subscriber has both SIM-card and phone. He remains a current subscriber until he changes his card (switcher), phone (replacement market) or both (new subscriber). In terms of sales, the New Phone-column is more relevant, as it contains those people willing to buy new phones, either with or without a new SIM-card.

7.1.3 Business for Mobile Retailers: Survival of the Fittest

Typically, independent mobile retailers look very similar and seem to offer almost identical products (see section 5.2). The interchangeability of their goods causes an incredibly high competition among them. Additionally, the retailers cannot join any general consortiums or syndicates that regulate the business and protect its members in case of litigation. These kinds of consortiums do not exist in the Philippine mobile market. Most retailers run their businesses isolated from each other. There is only little communication among the competitors, and arrangements or agreements are missing. As the margins are generally low, the unnamed principle is to grow or to die. Regarding the highly competitive and sometimes hostile conditions, a comparison with the "survival of the fittest"-theory from the famous scientist Charles Darwin[31] is applicable: Those unable to adapt to the ongoing business environment have a lower chance to survive than those able to. As a natural consequence, only the strongest (i.e. best adapting retailers) survive.

7.2 The Philippine Matrices for the Mobile Market

As already mentioned, the objective of the market analysis was to construct Philippine Matrices that contain the total number of shops in the market to reflect the local retail structure. In the following section as well as in section 8.2 and 9.2, these matrices are presented, subdivided into the market, the shop type, the shop size and the distribution channel. The data for all of the depicted matrices have been taken from the GfK Philippine Retailer Database and were further organized for analysis purposes.

7.2.1 The Philippine Matrix for Independent Mobile Shops

Table 3 shows the Philippine Matrix for the mobile market for independent shops in Manila. The number of shops for the universe and the sample as well as the coverage rate can be read from the cells of the table. The universe comprises the totality of all existing independent mobile retailers in Manila. The sample is the number of shops, which have already joined the GfK panel. The sample is used for projection purposes. The coverage rate is the quotient of these two indicators and is given in percent. Besides market and shop type, the matrix is further subdivided according to the shop size. Sizes are classified in relation to the number of units sold per month. XS shops sell up to 40 units a month, S shops between 40 and 100; M shops between 100 and 200, L shops between 200 and 500 and XL shops sell more than 500 units a month. Another subdivision refers to the distribution channel, by which the phones are finally sold. In the Philippines, mobile phones are only distributed by TCS (Telecommunication) shops.

Table 3: Number of shops in the mobile universe (Independent – TCS, Manila)

The mobile universe: Independent – TCS, Manila						
Shop Size	**XS**	**S**	**M**	**L**	**XL**	**Total**
Universe	385	411	53	13	1	863
Sample	16	13	5	3	0	37
Coverage Rate	4.2%	3.2%	9.4%	23.1%	0%	4.3%

First, the total number of shops draws attention. There are 863 independent retail shops selling mobiles in Manila. Also notable is the high number of XS and S shops. About 800 or more than 90% of the total independent mobile retailers are extra small or small (each about 45%). 6% of all shops have medium size, and there are only a few of large or extra large size. Obviously, the absolute majority of independent mobile retailers do not have much space to offer. Most of them look like the typical tiny retail shop described earlier, which sells one to three mobiles a day.

7.2.2 The Philippine Matrix for Organized Mobile Shops

Table 4 depicts the Philippine Matrix for the mobile market for organized shops. Its structure is similar to Table 3, but the values shown in the cells are different for this shop type. The universe consists of 20 different organized shops, all of which have several outlets. In the Philippine Matrix itself, every shop is counted as one, regardless of the number of outlets. Considering the outlets, the quantity is 179 for Manila. 60% of them are medium sized and 10% are small. Extra small and extra large do not exist. Organized mobile retailers tend to be larger than independent.

Table 4: Number of shops in the mobile universe (Organized – TCS, Manila)

The mobile universe: Organized – TCS, Manila (Number of outlets: 179)						
Shop Size	XS	S	M	L	XL	Total
Universe	0	2	12	6	0	20
Sample	0	2	12	6	0	20
Coverage Rate	/	100%	100%	100%	/	100%

7.3 Analysis of the Philippine Mobile Market

Comparing the two tables with the Philippine Matrices for the mobile market clearly displays the numerical superiority of the independent towards the organized shops. The number of independent retailers is almost five times higher (863 to 179). This unequal ratio can further be demonstrated by focusing on the relative percentage of both shop types, measured on the total of all mobile retailers (which is 863 plus 179 = 1,042). 82.8% (863 / 1,042) of all retailers are independent while the remaining 17.2% (179 / 1,042) are organized.

7.3.1 The Relation between the Number of Shops and the Market Share

However, the numerical superiority of independent retailers does not imply that their sales volume is equally superior. On the contrary, the market share of the two shop types in the mobile section is comparable. It comes to 55% for the independent and 45% for the organized shops. Therefore, the relation between the number of shops and the market share is not pro-portional in the mobile market. The relatively small quantity of organized shop outlets almost dominates half of the Philippine mobile market. This is mainly because the average organized retailer is bigger and has a higher sales volume than his independent competitor has.

There are several factors behind the numerous existences of small independent retailers in the country. One of the reasons lies in the Filipino foundation culture (see section 5.2). Philippine people prefer setting up their own business to being employed. Whenever they are capable of raising the smallest start-up capital, they will try to work in self-employment, hoping to make a fortune. This attitude might explain the large number of independent shops, especially in Manila. The phenomenon is not limited to the mobile market. The Philippine retailer conquers plenty of other markets as well, such as food and beverages, lotteries, audiovisuals and car supplies, among others. Their turnover is usually smaller than that of the bigger organized shops having several outlets and completely different business possibilities. The latter achieve a relatively higher market share.

7.3.2 The Positioning of the Mobile Market and Implications for GfK

Figure 5 shows a positioning matrix[32] for the mobile market. Two suitable underlying dimensions are "stability" (stable versus unstable) and "style" (modern versus conservative). As described earlier, the mobile market is classified as very modern and very unstable. On the one hand, it is exposed to frequent changes and a lot of motion, which makes it an unstable market. On the other hand, it mainly deals with stylish and trendy products and is therefore considered as modern.

Figure 5: A positioning matrix for the mobile market

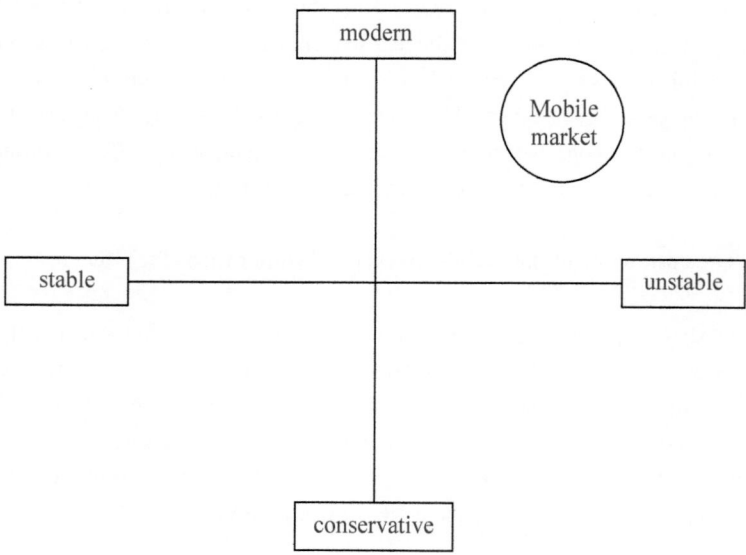

It is a central aim at GfK Philippines to persuade as many retailers as possible to join the GfK panel. The challenging circumstances of the Philippine mobile market complicate the efforts to meet that goal. One of the central problems is the instability of the market. Small handset shops may appear and vanish within days. Several reasons are likely to account for this remarkable instability, particularly that of the independent retail market: Tax evasion, frequent insolvencies and unexpected changes of the distributed product type. They all share the regrettable consequence that the existing collaboration with GfK Philippines is being interrupted or ended. However, one of the most important prerequisites for a mutually successful business relationship is permanent continuity. For GfK, data need to be collected regularly, not occasionally, to ensure the accuracy of projections.

Besides the unpleasant interruption of current business relations, a second aspect comes into focus: The complicated process of convincing the shops to initially join the GfK panel (see section 5.4). Local Filipinos, who do not care about abstract figures like specific sales volumes or competitors' market shares, own the majority of shops. They are just interested in selling their products with the highest profit possible. They do not recognise the potential benefits resulting from joining the GfK panel. Primarily, they feel controlled and uncomfortable and therefore hesitate or refuse to work with GfK.

Circumstances are somewhat different for the organized market. Most of the organized mobile retailers are either of medium or large size. Their higher turnover and their relatively higher market share indicate that the market structure is likely to be more stable. Besides, organized shops normally have several outlets. Even in the case that one of these goes bankrupt, GfK can at least still get the data from the other outlets and keep a good enough view of the sales of that retailer. Organized shops are less frequently subject to changes, which simplifies their recruitment and increases the possibility to keep them in the panel. It is realistic to expect an organized retailer to remain in business for a longer time than an independent one, which enhances the value of collaboration for GfK. Finally, organized shops (not their outlets) are not as interchangeable as independent ones. The former have different (strategic) business concepts, including the interior design of the stores and the range of distributed products. Due to all these reasons, it is particularly important for GfK to win all organized mobile retailers as clients.

Unfortunately, the necessity to recruit these retailers does not simplify the process itself. Some of the advantages mentioned above are not an issue until the retailers have joined the panel. The act of convincing them can be even more cost intensive compared to independent retailers. One major problem is to get an appointment with the shop owners or at least with the shop managers. As already explained for independent retailers, they are usually short on time and perhaps not willing to agree on appointments, the benefit of which is not clear to them in advance. It might take several trials to meet them. In the case there has been a successful first meeting with an employee from the shop, this employee usually must have a word with his boss first. The boss (often the shop manager) himself asks for another meeting with GfK in order to make up his own mind about GfK before reporting to the shop owner. Naturally, the shop owner also wants to know the people he is supposed to give highly sensitive sales data to. Meanwhile, GfK would already have three or more meetings without any guarantee that business cooperation will result. This typical sequence of events occurs in the process of recruiting organized shops. It is based on the retailers' hierarchical flow of information. The decision process itself is generally much faster with independent retailers.

-----

[24] Information taken from the GfK Asia E-News Letter, Philippine Edition, January 2005, Vol. 1, p. 8-10, 20-21.

[25] See "Motorola aims to regain lost footing in RP mobile market" (July 18, 2004) from Philippine Inquirer (http://www.inq7.net/inf/2004/jul/19/inf_4-1.htm).

[26] See analysis from GfK Philippines ("Phi MOB hitlist Jan 2005").

[27] Information taken from Telecom Direct News (http://www.telecomdirectnews.com/do.php/120/13815?29).

[28] For further reading, see Stephen Janson in *CommunicationsWeek International* (UK, EMAP), May 20, 2002.

[29] See Business World Online, Inc, Copyright 2002 (http://www.mobile-arts.com/news1.html).

[30] Information taken from Pyramid Research (http://www.pyramidresearch.com/pa_may12_phil.htm).

[31] See Charles Darwin, On the Origin of the Species (London: Murray, 1859).

[32] See Philip Kotler, Marketing Management, 11th edition (New Jersey: Prentice Hall, 2003), p. 537.

8. The Home Appliance Market in the Philippines

The topic of this part is the Philippine Home Appliance (HA) market. As in the previous chapter, the Philippine Matrices follow a general market description[33]. The last section contains the analysis and a positioning matrix for the HA market.

8.1 Description of the Philippine Home Appliance Market

The Philippine home appliance market is also called a *white goods market*. White goods or home appliances can generally be divided in two domains, namely *Major Domestic Appliances* (MDA) and *Small Domestic Appliances* (SDA). GfK currently tracks three products, which belong to MDA: Refrigerators, washing machines and air-conditioning. Typical SMA are microwaves, toasters and irons. GfK does not track them at present.

8.1.1 Market Overview: Current Competitors

The HA market is a brand-driven domain, occupied by many prestigious manufacturers competing each other[34]. Leading ones are Panasonic and Sharp from Japan, Whirlpool, Kelvinator and General Electric[35] from the United States and Samsung and Daewoo from South Korea. The refrigerator market is dominated by brands of American origin. Leading washing machine manufacturers are Japanese. Most appliances are produced outside the Philippines, mainly in Thailand and Malaysia, where production costs are lower. The Philippines' electricity and water costs, especially, belong to the highest in Asia.

Due to the relatively low purchasing power of the Filipinos (GDP per capita is below USD 1,000, see section 3.3), the whole HA market is generally directed and even dictated by the price. This is probably the main reason, why many local as well as other cheap Asian brands (especially Chinese) entered the market in the early 2000s. An example is the popular Philippine brand 3D. Most of them captured the low-end market, bringing about a great choice for consumers in that segment. In general, the quality of the low-priced goods is acceptable. There have been reports stating that most problems arise from the lack of support given to these products by their manufacturers.

Table 5, the top ten refrigerator sales in Manila of January 2005[36], shows that most units sold are low-end products between 110 to 140 Euro (prices have been converted). The only excep-tion is the Kolin KRD 70A, which costs only 70 Euro. Each of the dominant American brands like Kelvinator and General Electric sold approx. 20 refrigerators a day in January 2005.

Table 5: Hitlist of the top ten refrigerator sales in Manila (January 2005)

Rank	Model	Average Price (in Euro)	Quantities Sold
1	Kelvinator K 6SD	114	652
2	GE GAV 055BAPRLG / WW	130	568
3	Kelvinator KR070SDM	123	448
4	Sanyo SRS 70EW	134	442
5	Kolin KRD 70A	70	404
6	Panasonic NRA 704D	139	384
7	Sharp SJ 19T	125	367
8	Sanyo SRS 63EW	123	365
9	Panasonic NRA 704E	127	363
10	GE GAV 060BAPRLG/WW	139	321

8.1.2 Facts, Figures and Characteristics

The market still holds an enormous potential. The Philippines' penetration rates for white goods are low compared to other Asian countries. Many Filipino households, especially those in the greater provinces, are still not equipped with basic white goods like washing machines. The HA market is heavily concentrated in Manila, which constitutes about 15% of the total market (in terms of population). The remaining 85% are located in the rural provinces and on the islands in the south of the country. Table 6 illustrates the remarkable differences in penetration rates for Manila and the provinces. The percentage of refrigerators and washing machines in Manila is almost twice as high as outside the capital. When it comes to air-conditioning, it is even four times higher in the capital. The lower percentage of air-conditioning is probably due to the expensive Philippine electricity.

Table 6: Comparison of market penetration for white goods in Manila and the provinces

	Manila	**Outside the capital**
Refrigerators	60%	30-35%
Washing machines	60%	30-35%
Air-conditioning	20%	5%

Unlike the mobile market, the HA market can be described as stable. Because most of the white goods technology is already sufficiently matured, the number of newly invented features is significantly smaller than for other markets. However, the common classification of the HA market as calm and far behind may be biased. Some experts agree that the market is underestimated, supported by the absence of headlines and reports about it. The image of the HA market is very different from the mobile market. The latter is considered hot and trendy, with a lot of information being available and distributed automatically. Most Filipinos are probably able to recall more information about released cell phone models than recent technological

GfK

developments in washing machines. As there are more advertisements and commercials about mobiles, these are more salient to the consumers. However, the absence of news does not mean that there are no technological innovations in the HA market.

Despite the plainness of typical HA goods, the modern lifestyle in Manila requires families to at least have major domestic appliances. The greater challenge is to spread these products to the rural areas of the country where people's purchasing power is lower. Currently, only the best-positioned brands are able to move in these markets. Figure 6 illustrates that the annual growth rates for refrigerators and washing machines are between four and seven percent since 2002. From the late 90's until 2001, growth rates have been negative, indicating that fewer products have been sold. Since then, they have increased considerably.

Besides the Filipinos' brand awareness, they consider buying white goods as an investment and try to make full use of the lifespan. This behaviour cannot be generalized for other mar-kets. In the mobile market, consumers tend to change their handsets regularly. For the majority of the Filipinos, there seems to be no desire to proceed with white goods in the same way.

Figure 6: Growth rates for refrigerators and washing machine

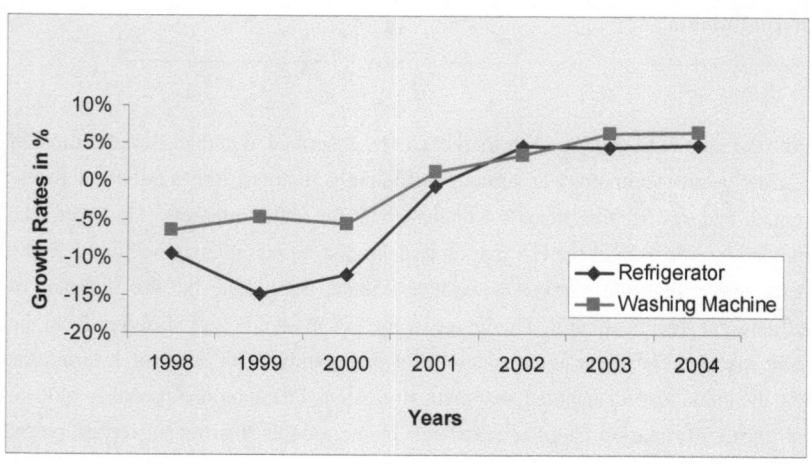

8.2 The Philippine Matrices for the Home Appliance Market

This section contains the Philippine Matrices for the HA market. A number of different distribution channels have to be distinguished in this market. It is possible to buy white goods at four different locations: *General Electric Shops* (GES), *White Good Stores* (WGS), *Department Stores* (DS) and *Hypermarkets* (HM). General electric shops sell all kinds of electrical appliances, including white and brown goods. This is the major difference to white good stores which sell (as implied by the name) white goods only. WGS are rather wholesalers than classical retailers, normally located outside Manila, serving clients with bigger orders. Department stores are stores offering a broad variety of items such as clothing, food, furniture and books. Hypermarkets mainly sell groceries and household articles (see section 2.2.2). The following Tables 7 to 9 contain the Philippine Matrices for independent and organized shops, subdivided into the four retail distribution channels explained above.

8.2.1 The Philippine Matrix for Independent HA Shops

Table 7 depicts the Philippine Matrix for the HA market for independent GES. The structure of the table is similar to the matrices shown in the previous chapter. Shops are classified into sizes from small to x-large according to turnover. Small shops make a turnover of max. 3,000 Philippine Pesos (44 Euro) a month, medium shops generate up to 7,000 Pesos (102 Euro), large shops max. 11,000 Pesos (160 Euro) and x-large ones generate a turnover of more than 11,000 Pesos a month.

GfK

Table 7: Number of shops in the HA universe (Independent – GES, Manila)

The HA universe: Independent – GES, Manila					
Shop Size	S	M	L	XL	Total
Universe	22	18	9	0	49
Sample	2	3	3	0	8
Coverage Rate	9%	17%	33%	/	16%

There are 49 independent GES in Manila. Eight out of these 49 have already joined the GfK panel, which corresponds to a coverage rate of 16%. With approx. 40% each, the small and medium sized independent shops are the most numerous representatives, followed by a 20% share of large shops. Obviously, there are only a relatively small number of independent shops selling white goods in Manila.

8.2.2 The Philippine Matrices for Organized HA Shops

Table 8 shows the number of organized general electric shops in the HA universe. There are 22 organized shops in Manila with a total of 156 outlets. More than 50% of them are small shops and less than 10% are x-large shops. The number of organized GES and the total number of outlets are comparable to those of organized mobile retailers (22 versus 20 shops; 156 versus 179 outlets). The number of independent HA retailers in Manila is much lower than for independent mobile retailers (49 versus 863). The huge difference between these two markets, which is observable for independent shops, vanishes for organized ones.

GfK

Table 8: Number of shops in the HA universe (Organized – GES, Manila)

The HA universe: Organized – GES, Manila (Number of outlets: 156)					
Shop Size	**S**	**M**	**L**	**XL**	**Total**
Universe	12	5	3	2	22
Sample	12	5	3	2	22
Coverage Rate	100%	100%	100%	100%	100%

The next table depicts the number of organized WGS, DS and HM from the HA universe. There are three different white good stores, two department stores and three hypermarkets currently operating in the capital. Their total number of outlets sums up to 45 (11 for WGS, 20 for DS and 14 for HM).

Table 9: Number of shops in the HA universe (Organized – WGS / DS / HM, Manila)

The HA universe: Organized – WGS / DS / HM, Manila (Number of outlets: 11 / 20 / 14)					
Shop Size	**S**	**M**	**L**	**XL**	**Total**
Universe / WGS	1	0	2	0	3
Sample / WGS	0	0	0	0	0
Coverage Rate /WGS	0%	/	0%	/	0%
Universe / DS	1	0	0	1	2
Sample / DS	0	0	0	1	1
Coverage Rate / DS	0%	/	/	100%	50%
Universe / HM	1	2	0	0	3
Sample / HM	1	2	0	0	3
Coverage Rate / HM	100%	100%	/	/	100%

8.3 Analysis of the Philippine Home Appliance Market

There are 250 HA shops in Manila. The coverage rate for organized shops is almost 87%. Approximately 80% of all shops are organized (201 of 250), the remaining 20% are independent (49 of 250). Obviously, the biggest volume of the capital's retail sales for home appliances occurs in organized distribution channels. For the past two years, a growing trend towards organized retailers targeting Metro Manila's middle to high-income group is observable. The faster development of the this retail channel has been supported by the city's 12 million consumers who have a purchasing power three to four times higher than the national average. Nowadays, independent shops only dominate the rural areas particularly outside the Luzon area. The low urbanization of this region hinders the progress of the retail sector. Most independent shops are single proprietorship and target the low-income groups of the population.

8.3.1 The Relation between the Number of Shops and the Market Share

The distribution of independent and organized shops in the HA market (49 versus 201) is pretty much opposite to the mobile market, in which more than 80% of all shops are independent. Another dissimilarity is that the 80% of organized shops in the HA market hold a corresponding market share of 80%. The relation between the number of shops and their market share is proportional in the white goods market. This relation does not apply to the mobile market, in which organized shops hold a far bigger than proportional market share (17% of all shops control 45% of the whole market).

8.3.2 The Positioning of the HA Market and Implications for GfK

As the distribution of shops between the HA and the mobile market is dissimilar, the conditions of both markets are likely to differ, too. Figure 7 depicts a positioning matrix for the mobile and HA market. Its dimensions are "stability" and "style" (see previous chapter). The HA market is classified in the opposite quadrant to that for the mobile market. The HA market is stable and conservative and might therefore be easier to control. It is more established, organized and not so frequently subject to changes. This is mainly due to the two reasons already mentioned:

1. The HA market mostly consists of organized shops, which are likely to be viable longer than independent ones.
2. Home appliances are steadier than mobiles and have a higher product life expectancy.

Additionally, Filipinos try to keep these appliances as long as possible. These factors have a calming effect on the market that prevents it from being as lively as the mobile market.

Figure 7: A positioning matrix for the mobile and HA market

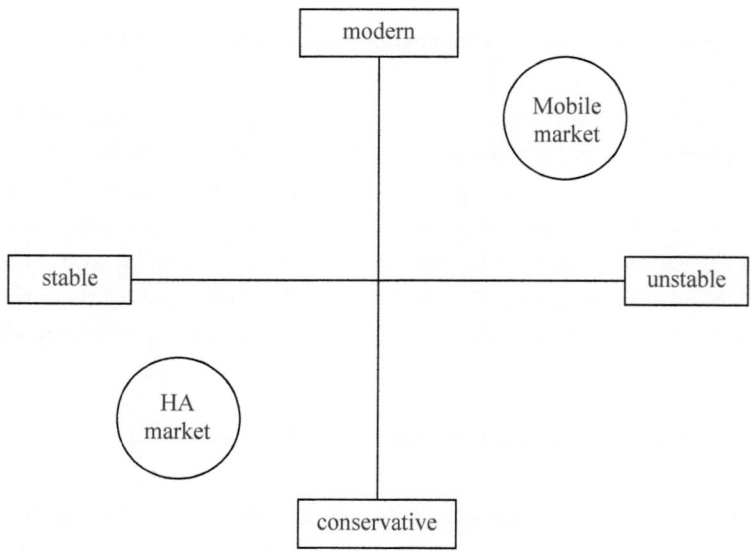

However, the characteristics of the HA market do not give rise to conclude that it is easier for GfK to initially enter that market. It can be even more difficult to influence the conservative HA retailers to venture to collaborate with GfK. As they are used to calm, rarely changing conditions, the GfK request could be surprising or too demanding to them. It is conceivable, that they react with even greater scepticism than mobile retailers do. The latter are used to turbulent conditions where good market information is more relevant for the daily business. They may be more earnest towards new challenges like the GfK proposal.

There are 250 HA and over 1,000 mobile shops in Manila. The Philippine retail market has four times more stores selling cell phones than white goods. This ratio is not evidence that HA retailers are less important, but merely a consequence of the manifold structure of the whole retail market. There are several explanations for the numerical superiority of mobile shops. The first is the tendency that Filipinos from the capital and from the rural areas prefer to buy mobiles to home appliances. This phenomenon can be referred to a particular attitude of these people: The higher the reputation of an item, the more likely it is to be bought. For Filipinos, it is important that goods are of high repute. As the status gained by the purchase of a smart phone is much higher than for white goods, they are likely to be bought more often. As a result of a given supply and demand-function, the number of mobile shops increases: The high demand of mobiles goes with a high supply of mobile shops. Respectively, the lower demand of home appliances goes with a lower supply of HA shops.

Another reason serving the principal of supply and demand is the cheaper entry possibility to the mobile market. As already shown in Table 1 (see page 34), the lowest rate for cell phones is about 50 Euro. Consumers have to pay twice this price for basic HA goods. Together with the people's weak purchasing power, this further explains the unequal existence of the two product types. This aspect can be viewed from the retailer's perspective as well. The harder entry conditions for the HA market mean a greater barrier to them, since they need a higher amount of money to invest in this business. Finally, it can be assumed that the target group for mobile phones is bigger than for home appliances. It is common that several people from the same household own a cell phone, whereas washing machines and refrigerators are usually shared among family members.

To sum up, the HA market mainly differs from the mobile market in regard to two points: First, there are four times more mobile shops than HA shops in Manila. This numerical difference results from the higher number of independent shops. The number of organized shops (and their outlets) is comparable in both markets. As most of the organized shops are general electric stores, it is sensible to particularly attend to this kind of stores. Second, the relation between the number of shops and their market share is proportional in the white goods market (the 80% majority of organized shops accounts for a market share of approx. 80%). In the mobile market, the 17% minority of organized shops holds a market share of 45%.

---

[33] Information taken from the GfK Asia E-News Letter, Philippine Edition, January 2005, Vol. 1, p. 10-14.

[34] For further reading, see "A classic Buyer's Market" in Asia Week 2001 (http://www.asiaweek.com/asiaweek/97/0502/biz4.html).

---

[35] Information taken from General Electric Philippines Homepage (http://www.ge.com/ph/appl.htm).

[36] See analysis from GfK Philippines (PHIL-REF-0404).

9. The Audio Visual Market in the Philippines

This chapter analyses the Philippine Audio Visual (AV) market. After a general description[37], the Philippine Matrices for the AV market will be presented. The last section contains the analysis and a positioning matrix for the AV market.

9.1 Description of the Philippine Audio Visual Market

The Philippine audio visual market covers all kind of electrical appliances, which function is to stimulate the audio or visual sense organ. GfK tracks six different products: Audio Home Systems (AHS, mainly hi-fi and Dolby Surround Systems), Cathode Ray Tubes (CRT, customary tube TVs), Plasma TVs (Projection TVs (PTV), Plasma and LCD-TVs), DVD Players, VCD Players and Camcorders.

9.1.1 Market Overview: Current Competitors

The Philippine AV market holds promising sales potentials. It offers an incredible choice of different appliances[38] from more than 25 various brands. Buyers are very brand conscious. The market is especially dominated by Japanese brands like Sony, Panasonic and Sharp. Second are Korean ones, e.g. Samsung and LG. Unknown trademarks of less value also found their place in the market. The majority of these are of Chinese origin, usually imported by Filipino dealers. VCD and DVD players from these no-name brands cost less than half the price of their branded counterparts from Japan or Korea. They only have very basic features, but are accepted more and more by the Filipinos.

Manufacturers' huge advertising campaigns contribute to the enormous influence of the world-famous brands dominating the Philippine AV market. Figure 8 gives an example of such a campaign run by Pioneer. Manufacturers permanently ensure that consumers are insistently encouraged to buy their shopping goods. Modern exhibitions, organized by local distributors and international manufacturers, are another popular way to influence the consumer's buying behaviour. A recent one

(December 13-30, 2004) has been conducted by "Automatic Center" (a local organized retailer) and Toshiba, Sony, LG, Philips, Samsung, Sharp and Panasonic. It was called "Plasma Pleasures, the Ultimate Entertainment Exhibit". During this big event, the audience was allowed to experience the latest plasma, LCD- and projection TVs in the country's first ever plasma show.

Figure 8: Advertising campaign from Pioneer

The following table depicts the hitlist of the top ten DVD player sales in Manila of January 2005[39]. The only unknown brand takes eighth place. The remaining nine positions are filled by international brands. Pioneer makes most devices from this hitlist. The average price for each unit is approx. 70 to 80 Euro (prices have been converted).

Table 10: Hitlist of the top ten DVD player sales in Manila (January 2005)

Rank	Model	Average Price (in Euro)	Quantities Sold
1	LG DV 8621P	71	1369
2	JVC XVN 312S	39	1339
3	Samsung DVDP 248K	77	1229
4	Pioneer DV 270S	78	1124
5	Sony DVPNS 575P	84	1070
6	Pioneer DV 366	78	986
7	Pioneer DV 373S	80	943
8	Nextbase NB 787S	57	919
9	Sharp DVSL 8	83	918
10	Philips DVD 320	70	915

9.1.2 Facts, Figures and Characteristics

The current section provides a description of the status quo of the six AV products tracked by GfK. There happens to be a continuous decline in the demand for audio home systems. This trend is supposed to be related to the significantly increased demand for the portable and lower-priced MP3 format players. A second reason for the diminished demand for AHS is the growing spread of DVD players. The tremendous increase in demand for this type of disc format in Metro Manila can mainly be attributed to three factors: First, DVD players are cheaper than regular CD players and audio home systems. Second, there is a greater choice of manufacturers (and brands) available. Third, DVD players are equipped with additional functions, allowing users to play CDs, VCDs, S-VCDs and MPEG formats. As a result, the conventional CD player becomes unnecessary and consumers welcome the opportunity to save on one electrical appliance. The demand for CD players and AHS has shrunk considerably. Predictions for 2005 do not suggest any recovery. This is quite opposite to the German market, which has not experienced a strong decline in AHS demand. German consumers still prefer to buy separate audio and DVD appliances.

The demand for VCD players is also falling away. Especially in Manila, the abundance of DVD format media and DVD players is overwhelming and does not leave much market share for VCD players. The DVD market has enjoyed growth rates in excess of 150% per year at the expense of the VCD market, thus tipping the scales clearly in its own favour. The bigger growth rates for DVD players are further supported by the appearance of low entry-level Chinese brands priced almost like VCD players. The DVD is the major format with no equivalent competitor. The two potential followers, the blue-ray-disc and the hd-DVD format are not common in the country at present. The penetration rate of DVD players is 70% for Manila and 60% for the rest of the country. There are still regions in the Philippines where the only available disc format is the VCD. The penetration rate for VCD players is lower than for DVD players.

Another product type tracked by GfK Philippines is the CRT-Television, the conventional tube TV. The largest piece of turnover generated in the AV field comes from this product category (DVD players are ranked second). CRT-Televisions exist in a curved and a flat version. Conventional curved and flat TVs are comparable in prices, since they offer the same picture quality only by using different tube forms. The trend clearly points towards flat TVs, which had a market share of 60% in 2004 (40% taken by curved TVs). Predictions for 2005 see flat TVs consolidating their lead over curved ones, achieving an 80% to 20% relation. At present the majority of customers for CRT in Metro Manila rank Japanese brands first, with Sony being the leading manufacturer, followed closely by Sharp. The 21-inch CRT is the most marketable screen size. Penetration rates for TVs are 60% in Manila and 50% outside.

In comparison to CRT TVs, plasma TVs (PTV, plasma and LCD-TVs) are categorized as high-end appliances. They are still expensive and rarely available outside Manila. However, substantial price reductions for these sophisticated goods would certainly create more demand. The reputation of the pricey LCD-TVs has been exposed to some damage lately: Several cases of appliances with dead pixels made consumers perceive LCD technology as not yet matured. Buyers have asked for replacements and refunds, not realizing that dead pixels do not mean the PTV is defective or malfunctioning. However, the image of these high-end appliances has been scathed.

The last audited product from the audio visual market is the camcorder. It currently enjoys great popularity in Manila. Photo and video have always been an integral part of the Filipino, who loves to capture (parts of) his life either on photo or video. Because of the expensive prices for camcorders in the past, the demand was low. After they have dropped, there is a noticeable increase in sales.

A common incentive that dealers and retailers frequently offer their customers is the interest-free bid[40]. By purchasing any high-end appliance, users are likely to receive a six or twelve interest-free months promotion, valid for major credit cards. This enables them to buy expensive items at equal monthly instalments at zero percent interest. Due to the high acceptance of this payment option, a majority of high-end sales is completed by credit card.

9.2 The Philippine Matrices for the Audio Visual Market

There are four different retail distribution channels in the AV market audited by GfK. Three of them have already been introduced at the home appliance market: General Electric Shops (GES), Department Stores (DS) and Hypermarkets (HM). The fourth channel is called *Audio Visual Shops* (AVS). A variety of audio visual products can be purchased there. In the following, the Philippine Matrices for independent and organized retailers are presented, subdivided into the four retail distribution channels relevant for the AV market.

9.2.1 The Philippine Matrix for Independent AV Shops

Table 11 depicts the Philippine Matrix for the AV market for independent audio visual shops and general electric shops. AVS are classified into sizes from small to x-large according to monthly turnover (small shops: 0 to 700 Philippine Pesos (0-10 Euro), medium shops: 700 to 2,000 Pesos (10-29 Euro), large shops: 2,000 to 7,000 Pesos (29-102 Euro), x-large shops: More than 7,000 Pesos a month).

Table 11: Number of shops in the AV universe (Independent – AVS / GES, Manila)

The AV universe: Independent – AVS / GES, Manila					
Shop Size	**S**	**M**	**L**	**XL**	**Total**
Universe / AVS	73	71	39	0	183
Sample / AVS	9	7	6	0	22
Coverage Rate / AVS	12%	10%	15%	/	12%
Universe / GES	22	18	9	0	49
Sample / GES	2	3	3	0	8
Coverage Rate / GES	9%	17%	33%	/	16%

As shown in the table, there are 232 independent AV retailers in Manila, 183 AVS and 49 GES. 12% of the AVS and 16% of the GES have already joined the GfK panel. Almost 80% of the independent AVS are small or medium sized, the remaining 20% are large. This ratio also applies for the GES. Neither of these distribution channels has x-large stores. In relation to the number of independent shops (232), the AV market takes up a medium position compared with the mobile (863) and HA (49) markets.

9.2.2 The Philippine Matrices for Organized AV Shops

Table 12 contains the number of organized AVS / GES in the AV universe. There are four organized audio visual shops in Manila with a total of 21 outlets. Half of them are medium sized, half x-large. The universe also contains 22 organized GES with a total of 156 outlets. About 50% of them are small sized. Coverage rate is 100% for both shop types. The last Philippine Matrix is presented in Table 13. It shows the number of organized department stores and hypermarkets in the AV universe. There are two DS and three HM, with 20 and 14 outlets, respectively.

Table 12: Number of shops in the AV universe (Organized – AVS / GES, Manila)

The AV universe: Organized – AVS / GES, Manila (Number of outlets: 21 / 156)					
Shop Size	**S**	**M**	**L**	**XL**	**Total**
Universe / AVS	0	2	0	2	4
Sample / AVS	0	2	0	2	4
Coverage Rate / AVS	/	100%	/	100%	100%
Universe / GES	12	5	3	2	22
Sample / GES	12	5	3	2	22
Coverage Rate / GES	100%	100%	100%	100%	100%

Table 13: Number of shops in the AV universe (Organized – DS / HM, Manila)

The AV universe: Organized – DS / HM, Manila (Number of outlets: 20 / 14)					
Shop Size	**S**	**M**	**L**	**XL**	**Total**
Universe / DS	1	0	0	1	2
Sample / DS	0	0	0	1	1
Coverage Rate / DS	0%	/	/	100%	50%
Universe / HM	1	2	0	0	3
Sample / HM	1	2	0	0	3
Coverage Rate / HM	100%	100%	/	/	100%

9.3 Analysis of the Philippine Audio Visual Market

The total number of organized shops in the AV universe is 211. The AV market has almost an equal number of independent and organized shops (232 versus 211). It is the only one of the three studied markets having a well-balanced ratio of shop types (52% to 48%). The number of organized shops in the AV market is comparable to those in the HA market. These two markets only differ in the number of their independent shops (232 to 49, respectively). This makes the AV market bigger than the HA market. Circumstances are similar in the comparison of the AV and mobile markets. These two also have numbers of organized shops in the same order of magnitude (232 versus 179) and distinguish themselves by their independent shops, since there are four times more independent mobile than AV shops in Manila. With more than 1,000 retailers, the mobile market is the biggest one, followed by the AV market with 443 and the HA market with 250 shops.

9.3.1 The Relation between the Number of Shops and the Market Share

In Metro Manila, the market share for every audited product (except VCD players) is bigger for organized shops (see Table 14). The average market share for AV products amounts to 72.5% for organized retailers, leaving 27.5% for independent ones. The shares for organized retailers selling plasma TVs or camcorders are clearly higher than this average value. The only exception is VCD players, for which the sales volume is mainly controlled by independent shops (60% to 40%). Despite the equal number of independent and organized shops in the AV market, the market share for both shop types is different. The 48% of organized shops hold a market share of 72.5%. This ratio is because organized shops are usually bigger and profit from a higher sales volume. They can defend their superior market position because consumers seem to prefer to buy their AV goods in these more sophisticated, exclusive stores. Additionally, some manufacturers favour organized shops because they do not want their prestigious products to be sold next to hundreds of counterfeits or Chinese low-end products.

The greater strength of organized shops is already known from the mobile market, where less than 20% of all shops in the universe control almost 45% of the market. This relation is not repeated in the HA market, which shows a proportional market share of its organized shops (80% of the universe control 80% of the market). The market shares for the AV and HA markets are quite similar (72.5% and 80%) for organized shops.

Today's high sales volume of Manila's organized shops does not match the past situation at all. Fifteen to twenty years ago, the AV market was clearly dominated by independent shops. It was very common to purchase CD players and TVs at one of the countless and widespread independent retailers, especially in the Raon area, the former electronics center of Manila. This was prior to the emergence of bigger organized retailers, whose prices could compete with those from Raon. Slowly but steadily, the dominant position of the independent retailers was broken up. They could only watch as the more convenient organized stores occupied the market. People became more and more attracted by the opportunity to do their shopping in one of the huge malls that were built all over the city. Besides competitive prices, the worry- free shopping conditions (fewer robbers and muggers), the attractive merchandize displays, convenient parking lots and other value-added services made this shift happen. As Raon's independent retailers could not stop this development, today's audio visual market is clearly ruled by organized shops.

Table 14: Comparison of market share between independent and organized shops for different goods in the AV market

	Independent	Organized
CRT (tube TVs)	20%	80%
Plasma TV (PTV / LCD-TVs)	10%	90%
AHS (Audio Home Systems)	30%	70%
VCD Player	60%	40%
DVD Player	30%	70%
Camcorder	15%	85%
Average	**27.5%**	**72.5%**

9.3.2 The Positioning of the AV Market and Implications for GfK

Figure 9 contains a positioning matrix for all three markets. Whereas the mobile and HA markets are positioned oppositely, the AV market takes up a place between them. It receives medium values on both dimensions "stability" and "style". The AV market is neither unstable nor stable. Furthermore, it is neither particularly conservative nor modern. It is therefore placed in the centre of Figure 9, in which the axes of the two dimensions cross each other. This positioning implies, that the AV market is less conservative (more modern) than the HA market. This assumption seems to be reasonable: DVD players or camcorders are trendier products than washing machines or refrigerators. Additionally, the former are not bought because of practical reasons only. It is interesting that even the poor Filipinos from rural areas prefer to buy AV rather than HA goods, even if the latter serve practical purposes to a higher degree. Finally, the AV market is more driven by technology and innovations. However, as it is more subject to change, it is at the same time less stable than the HA market. The product life cycle is generally faster for DVD players or camcorders than for washing machines, indicating that new products need to be developed more often to remain profitable.

Figure 9: A positioning matrix for the mobile, HA and AV market

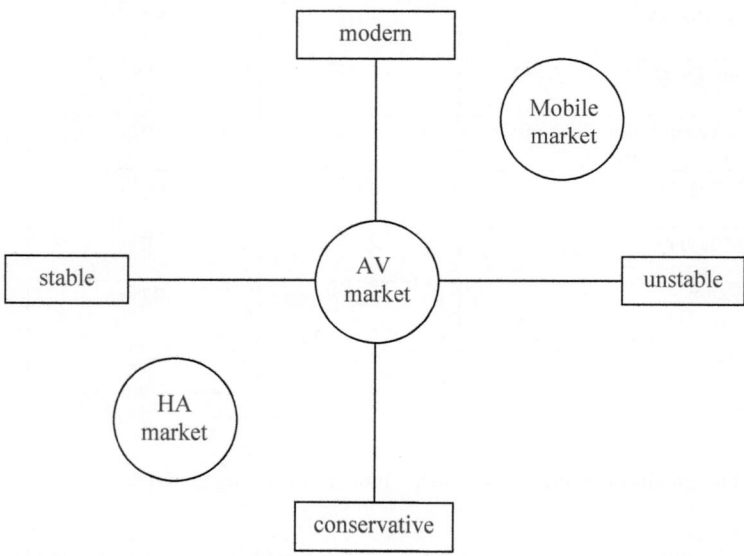

The central positioning of the AV market further implies, that it is more conservative (less modern) than the mobile market. This statement seems realistic, too. As already described, the mobile market is currently one of the Philippines' hottest markets. Its products are very modern, strongly technology-driven and replaced by the future generation within weeks. Compared to these circumstances, the AV market is classified more conservative. Simultaneously, it is more stable. People do not change their brown goods as often as their mobile handsets. Due to these considerations, the positioning of the AV market in the middle of the two others seems appropriate.

To conclude, the AV market holds a distinct position in comparison to the other two with regard to the following points: First, the AV market is the only market with a well-balanced ratio of independent and organized shops. Second, its total number of shops (443) lies between those of the mobile and HA markets (1,042 and 250, respectively). Third, all three markets have a corresponding number of organized shops, but due to its number of independent shops, the AV market can be considered bigger than the HA but smaller than the mobile market. Fourth, as almost 80% of the independent shops in the AV market are AVS shops, it is recommended to particularly attend to that distribution channel.

---

[37] Information taken from the GfK Asia E-News Letter, Philippine Edition, January 2005, Vol. 1, p. 15-19.

[38] For further reading, see Department of Trade & Industry (http://www.dti.gov.ph/contentment/9/16/20/233.jsp).

[39] See analysis from GfK Philippines (JANHITLIST-DVD).

[40] See "A classic Buyer's Market" in Asia Week 2001 (http://www.asiaweek.com/asiaweek/97/0502/biz4.html).

10. Recommendations for the GfK Management

This chapter provides recommendations for the GfK Management, which have been derived from the previous analysis of the three business markets. Since GfK has only been represented on the Philippines for 12 months the company still needs to enhance its market awareness and win new clients. Consequently, suggestions focus primarily on the recruitment of retailers and on marketing communications measures. Implications of the Philippine retail structure according to the GfK Methodology have been discussed in section 5.4.

The possibilities to manage the low-developed Philippine retail market are somewhat limited. As mentioned, it is often difficult to convince retailers from the general proposal of GfK, especially at the early stages of contact. To underline that the cooperation is mutually beneficial, emphasizing resulting short-term advantages is suggested. As these are immediately noticeable, they may help to let the GfK idea appear more promising than by focusing only on long-term rewards. Suitable points to mention could be that participating retailers are always fully aware of their sales volumes. With the regular filling in of the GfK data sheets, some parts of their accounting become redundant because they are already done on a regular basis. Best and worst selling-products are determined as well, which allows the deduction of well-founded supply decisions.

Besides coming up with good arguments, developing an amicable relationship with the decision-makers (usually the shop owners) and the employees is extremely important. In the Philippines and in other Asian countries everything is about relationships. Arrangements and deals are easier to realize when the people involved act on a personal and harmonious basis. Similarly, retailers having a good relationship with GfK are more likely to cooperate with the company.
Although this aspect is well known, it is not easy to put into practice. The development of intensive relationships requires time and well-considered actions. However, time is the thing missing most in retail business. Driven by competitive forces, shop owners and employees are usually very busy. They have to take care of

their clients, stay in contact with wholesale dealers and suppliers, handle the administrative paperwork and keep the shop well ordered. When employees from GfK come by to introduce their company, it is unlikely that they have time to talk to them right away; and it takes even more time to develop a more binding relationship.

In addition to the previous considerations, GfK should plan several visits to each shop. A greater number of meetings will intensify the contact and increase the possibility of mutual sympathy. In Asia, this process can be accelerated by the donation of small gifts. The handover of presents like calendars, cups or alarm clocks underlines one's good intentions. GfK Philippines also respects this practice and brings along small gifts whenever visiting (potential) clients. It is good advice to keep this habit to support the development of friendships. The donation of gifts is by no means sufficient to build or maintain a business relationship, but it supports the effects of other efforts.

In order to enhance its market awareness, which helps GfK to bind regular and win new clients, the company is well advised to exhaust several of the five modes of marketing communications[41]. A first mode is the classical advertising. GfK could (through advertising agencies) create print ads, which could be published in leading newspapers (e.g. the Philippine Inquirer), magazines (e.g. the Manila Bulletin) and journals related to its monitored business markets. It is also possible to think of online advertisements, preferably placed on frequently visited web pages (e.g. www.philippinebusiness.com). Another option is that of brochures and booklets from GfK Philippines. Either these could be sent directly to potential clients or they could be made available at important government and business institutions, e.g. the Philippine Chamber of Commerce or the Philippine Embassy. GfK should keep the official company logo to preserve corporate identity and refer its clients to the worldwide activities of the GfK Group. TV and broadcast advertisements are probably less suitable, as they are too expensive and the contact to the target group is not assured.

A second marketing communications mode is the personal selling. Transferred to a service company this includes the participation at fairs, trade shows and exhibitions related to the tracked markets. The major advantage of these communications channels is the gathering of a high number of potential clients, who can easily be addressed for recruiting purposes. GfK should participate as a visitor first. In case this is worthwhile, the company could become an exhibitor. Exhibitions organized by manufacturers (e.g. consumer electronics) can also be visited for the same reasons. Furthermore, the country's numerous shopping centres and malls can be used to hold company presentations and to set up information points about the business of GfK. This might be rewarding because many targeted retailers can be met there.

A third communications mode is called public relations and publicity. GfK certainly needs to care about its public perception and further improve its image. Press kits should be created in order to wait on the local media. Annual reports, company magazines and publications are other useful tools to convey an appropriate picture of the company to the public. GfK could engage itself in sponsorships, e.g. for sporting events, social topics or start-up enterprises. Seminars or speeches about subjects like the Philippine business markets or the Philippine retail structure can be offered as well. GfK could also invite potential and regular clients to special open-door events, which could be named "GfK Day" or something similar. During these informal meetings, GfK could present latest company news in combination with individual offerings for clients. If the local press is invited, this would also be a good opportunity to improve community relations.

The last communications mode mentioned here is the direct marketing. GfK Philippines is advised to continue writing regular (E-)Newsletters to inform clients and interested parties about actual performances, intentions and visions of the company. It is reasonable to offer clients a quarterly issue. Additionally, specific mailings in combination with advertising letters are another good method to attract the attention of well-chosen clients. Finally, the communications channel of telemarketing (fax and telephone) also represents an effective way to keep in touch with regular clients.

It can generally be recommended to GfK that it is mostly important to audit as many organized shops as possible. Organized shops hold a bigger market share than their independent competitors in two of the analysed markets (mobile and AV). It is more effective to track shops with a higher market share first to get an overview about a certain market. As these are more likely to be organized shops, it is essential for GfK to win them as clients.

GfK continuously has to face the challenging conditions of the retail structure in the Philippine markets. There will always be obstacles to overcome to further ensure the company's already promising position in the country. Fortunately, GfK's rising degree of recognition in Manila will facilitate the recruitment of new retailers in the future.

---

[41] See Philip Kotler, Marketing Management, 11th edition (New Jersey: Prentice Hall, 2003), p. 564.

11. Bibliography

1. Geoff Easton, Market Forms and Market Models (Lancaster University Managemet School Working Paper, 2004, http://www.lums.co.uk/publications), p. 1.

2. William G. Zikmund and Michael d'Amico, Effective Marketing. Creating and Keeping Customers, 2nd edition (Cincinnati: South-Western College Publishing Company, 1998), p. 8.

3. http://en.wikipedia.org/wiki/Market_forms

4. Philip Kotler, Swee H. Ang, Siew M. Leong and Chin T. Tan, Marketing Management, An Asian Perspective, 3rd edition (Singapore: Prentice Hall, 2003), chapter 4.

5. David Jobber, Principles and Practice of Marketing, 4th edition (Berkshire: McGraw-Hill, 2004), chapter 9.

6. Ron Hasty and James Reardon, Retail Management (USA: McGraw-Hill, 1997), p. 10.

7. Linda G. Poloian, Retailing Principles. A global Outlook (USA: Fairchild Publications, Inc., 2003), p. 8.

8. Barry Berman and Joel R. Evans, Retail Management. A Strategic Approach, 8th edition (New Jersey: Prentice Hall, 2001), p. 3.

9. Peter J. McGoldrick, Retail Marketing (Berkshire: McGraw-Hill, 1990), p. 63.

10. http://de.wikipedia.org/wiki/Philippinen

11. http://www.cia.gov/cia/publications/factbook/geos/rp.html#Intro

12. http://www.philippinebusiness.com.ph/guide/prc00.htm

13. GfK Asia E-News Letter, Philippine Edition, January 2005, Vol. 1, p. 11.

14. http://www.gfk.com

15. GfK Non-Food Tracking Brochure (2003)

16. GfK Asia Retail Service Version (August 2004)

17. GfK Asia Corporate Presentation (August 2004)

18. Andreas Hanslauer, *GfK: Champions League* (Focus Money, July 20, 2005), p. 16-17.

19. GfK Retail Service Presentation (February 2005)

20. http://www.oanda.com/convert/classic

21. http://www.dti.gov.ph/contentment/9/63/281.jsp

22. http://www.philembassy.au.com/download/nvestop_retail.pdf

23. "Construction of P500-M SM-Clark starts" (The Manila Times, March 29, 2005), http://www.manilatimes.net/national/2005/mar/29/yehey/prov/20050329pro5.html

24. GfK Asia E-News Letter, Philippine Edition, January 2005, Vol. 1, p. 8-10, 20-21.

25. "Motorola aims to regain lost footing in RP mobile market" (*The Philippine Inquirer*, July 18, 2004), http://www.inq7.net/inf/2004/jul/19/inf_4-1.html

26. Analysis from GfK Philippines ("Phi MOB hitlist Jan 2005").

27. http://www.telecomdirectnews.com/do.php/120/13815?29

28. Stephen Janson in *CommunicationsWeek International* (UK: EMAP), May 20, 2002.

29. Business World Online, Inc (Copyright 2002), http://www.mobile-arts.com/news1.html

30. http://www.pyramidresearch.com/pa_may12_phil.htm

31. Charles Darwin, *On the Origin of the Species* (London: Murray, 1859).

32. Philip Kotler, Marketing Management, 11th edition (New Jersey: Prentice Hall, 2003), p. 537.

33. GfK Asia E-News Letter, Philippine Edition, January 2005, Vol. 1, p. 10-14.

34. "A classic Buyer's Market", *Asia Week* 2001, http://www.asiaweek.com/asiaweek/97/0502/biz4.html

35. http://www.ge.com/ph/appl.htm

36. Analysis from GfK Philippines (PHIL-REF-0404).

37. GfK Asia E-News Letter, Philippine Edition, January 2005, Vol. 1, p. 15-19.

38. http://www.dti.gov.ph/contentment/9/16/20/233.jsp)

39. Analysis from GfK Philippines (JANHITLIST-DVD).

40. "A classic Buyer's Market", *Asia Week 2001*, http://www.asiaweek.com/asiaweek/97/0502/biz4.html

41. Philip Kotler, *Marketing Management*, 11th edition (New Jersey: Prentice Hall, 2003), p. 564.

Appendix A: Interview Guide

1. How many Shops do you run?

2. Where are they located (inside Metro Manila or outside)?

3. How about the sales in 2004?

4. What are your best-selling products?

5. What are consumers asking for most regularly?

6. In general, do you know exactly what your customer wants? What kind of problems may exist?

7. Did you notice the influence of the Chinese market? Are you selling Chinese products, too? How many percent of your total sales are due to Chinese products? Is there a difference in the quality?

8. How is your relationship with your manufacturer / supplier? What do you expect from a manufacturer / supplier?

9. For **independent** shops: Do you notice the influence from **organized** shops? / For **organized** shops: Do you notice the influence from **independent** shops?

10. What is your strongest wish concerning your business in 2005?

Appendix B: Choice of Given Answers in Interviews

Question 4: What are your best-selling products?

- Nokia 7610

- Brand new cell phones, most of it all: Nokia 7200 / Samsung E600 / SonyEricsson P900

- Mainly mobiles, only very few accessories / Nokia is number one brand

- Cell phones, mostly Nokia 3310 / 3315, probably because they are easy to repair, because the patches are available everywhere. Then models from Samsung, Sony-Ericsson and Motorola

- Amplifiers, Speakers, DVD players

- DVD and VCD players

- Colour TV

Question 5: What are consumers asking for most regularly?

- Nokia phones in general

- Colour TVs or DVD players

- For very cheap items between 1.850 and 2.700 Pesos (about 26 to 38 €)

Question 6: In general, do you know exactly what your customer wants? What kind of problems may exist?

- Difficult sometimes, as they try to bargain to put the price down

- Can handle the situation normally… but sometimes difficult, when there are reclama-tions, because fixing the phones is difficult, can only assist them

- Problem when I cant give them / sell them what they want, because they can go to another shop, and no cash for me

- Yes, it is very easy. I can observe him and find out about him.

- Not always, sometimes they come in and ask for a TV, without knowing the price and the features they need

- Models with a build-in camera, often from the low end of the high-tech-market, like the Motorola 6651

- Sometimes customers do not talk, and they get irritated, so you better leave them alone, and let them look around… they will be less shy then.

- Usually easy. We ask them what they would like to have. Of course, there are exceptions.

Question 7: Did you notice the influence of the chinese market?
Are you selling chinese products, too?
How many percent of your total sale are due to chinese products?
Is there a difference in the quality?

- I do notice the Chinese market influence. The quality from china is very good already, very competitive, customers do not care which country their cell phone is from, as long as it is cheap.

- The Chinese market is very noticeable here. All products are made in china already, also with cell phones. It is the same cell phones, even more extras included from those manufactured in china.

- The Chinese market is already strong, and the products are all right in general.

- Somehow noticeable – most products are from china, anyway – but the quality is different, sometimes worse, sometimes better.

- Did notice this influence! Chinese brands are cheaper, but also a bit worse, too! But people still prefer "original" brands normally.

- Of course, everything is from china now…especially the accessories, they are really cheaper. But the quality is different: there are "A-products" (second to the original) and "B-products" (cheaper ones in plastic packages only), both are from china. Difference in accessories is about 1000 Pesos, in phones about 4000 Pesos between china and original product (about 13,50 and 53,50 €, respectively).

- Brands like Nokia / Motorola are all manufactured in china, but people still like them to be manufactured in Finland or wherever, as they sometimes think the quality is higher there. So I don't tell customers their products are from china, as they may think twice about buying it. So we try to avoid any hesitating.

GfK

Continued from Question 7:

- Of course there is... it is lower prices then, compared to the other products. Sometimes the quality is good, and still less expensive than the brand products.

- Chinese products are so cheap... we see the Chinese influence, because we sometimes cannot sell our products. And there are a lot of new products from china, too. But those with higher quality have higher prices, too.

Question 8: How is your relationship with your supplier / wholesale dealer? What do you expect from a supplier / wholesale dealer?

- Sometimes difficult, as the price is to haggle about... sometimes that is differences about 200 Pesos only (2.70 €). I expect low prices and good service from a supplier, and a good delivery service.

- Business friends only... the dealer has to be responsible for any bad or faulty goods.

- Not so good, sometimes the goods are late, but there is no price reduction. That is not so comfortable.

- Good. We expect him to offer enough new products and good quality of course.

- Sometimes good, sometimes bad... good, because always in time, bad, because too expensive.

- It is ok, sometimes problems with the batteries. I expect good quality of course and competitive price.

GfK

Continued from Question 8:

- Good relationship and no barriers for the last 6 years. They need to provide me with the merchandise support; we are in contact almost every day. Problems arise if there isn't enough stock available.

- It is different now. Before, there was a nice relationship. Now, they do not take care of my profit any more... less service, too. And it is a problem to talk to the owner, they are hardly ever available, you just get representatives to talk to.

- Suppliers all are Chinese, that is good as we are Chinese, too. We expect them to deliver good quality only, as there will be less hustle with the customer afterwards. And we expect them to tell us when the price is down, so that we can copy the market.

Question 9: For independent shops: Do you notice the influence from
organized shops?

- No fear of organized shops. In the independent business, you don't have to share your profits, it is all for you only.

- No influence, the market is very wide, very tough competition tough.

- A lot of organized shops, but still enough customers here... ok.

- We sell the products at lower prices, so we do not have to fear them.

- Yes, there is a fear of these organized shops, as they have many branches, high volumes, and you can pay with credit card there. So it depends on the customer, if he feels inconvenient, he will not come to the independent shops any more.

- No fear of shopping malls... prices is still lower here, because the shopping malls usually cannot buy their stuff directly from the suppliers.

Question 9: For organized shops: Do you notice the influence from
independent shops?

- No, not at all, because we are already a national company and the independent ones are just too small to compete us now.

- No, not really. It is a better choice here, we have longer guarantees and people with more money are coming here.

- We are helping each other, no threat! Some customers prefer the small independent shops, as they are cheaper.

IEWS-Schriftenreihe, fortgesetzt ab Band 25 als „Schriftenreihe des ESB Research Institute"

1. *Tanja Henne*
   Derivative Finanzinstrumente und ihre Bilanzierung nach HGB, US-GAAP und IAS
   ISBN 3-8265-7830-9, Shaker-Verlag, Aachen

2. *Senol Agac*
   TV-Banking - Implications of a new delivery channel for financial services companies in Germany
   ISBN 3-8265-7831-7, Shaker-Verlag, Aachen

3. *Julia Pracht*
   Strategic Financing of Small- and Medium-Sized Enterprises in the German IT Sector
   ISBN 3-8265-7832-5, Shaker-Verlag, Aachen

5. *Andreas Resch*
   Valuation of Internet Companies - Difficult or Impossible?
   ISBN 3-8265-7834-1, Shaker-Verlag, Aachen

6. *Lars Herold*
   Public vs. Private Companies in Germany
   Quantifying, Understanding, and Closing the Performance Gap
   ISBN 3-8265-7835-X, Shaker-Verlag, Aachen

7. *Alexander Zimmer*
   Unternehmenskultur und Cultural Due Diligence bei Mergers & Acquisitions
   ISBN 3-8265-9118-6, Shaker-Verlag, Aachen

8. *Claudia Schulze, Verena Pfeiffer, Torsten Witzke*
   Aktives Kreditrisikomanagement: Portfoliomodelle & innovative Produkte
   ISBN 3-8265-9117-8, Shaker-Verlag, Aachen

9. *Pilar Zumft Cortines*
   Welthandel und Umweltschutz:
   Das Spannungsfeld von Welthandelsorganisation und Nichtregierungsorganisationen
   ISBN 3-8265-9163-1, Shaker-Verlag, Aachen

10. *Jonathan Labin*
    Erfolgsfaktoren elektronischer B2B-Marktplätze im Finanzdienstleistungssektor
    ISBN 3-8265-9164-X, Shaker-Verlag, Aachen

21. *Sonia Pereiro Méndez*
   "Equity carve out" als Desinvestitionsinstrument zur Steigerung des
   Unternehmenswertes
   ISBN 3-8322-2046-1, Shaker-Verlag, Aachen

22. *Sabine Weissinger*
   Realoptionen als Bewertungsansatz für Wachstumsunternehmen
   ISBN 3-8322-2121-2, Shaker-Verlag, Aachen

23. *Jörg Adams*
   Applicability of Real Option Valuation for High-Risk Investments
   ISBN 3-8322-2336-3, Shaker-Verlag, Aachen

24. *Sebastian Schienle*
   Die Anwendung der Theorie des Rent-Seeking auf einzelwirtschaftliche
   Unternehmensformen
   ISBN 3-8322-2629-X, Shaker-Verlag, Aachen

European School of Business

Undergraduate Studies: Wir messen uns nur mit den Besten

- Vier Jahre Studium, davon die Hälfte im Ausland
- Abgestimmte Lehr- und Prüfungsinhalte mit Partnerhochschulen
- Praxisnähe des Studiums
- Zwei Praxissemester, davon mindestens eines im Ausland
- Aktive Studentenschaft

Postgraduate Studies: Vertiefungen in Theorie und Praxis

Der MBA für internationale Kompetenz

- Präsenzstudium 3 Semester, Teilzeitstudium max. 3 Jahre
- Traditionsreichster MBA-Studiengang in Deutschland
- FIBAA Akkreditierung
- Modularer Aufbau des Studienganges
- Kleine, internationale und interdisziplinäre Gruppen

MSc: Academic quality at its best

- Drei Semester Studium; Abschluss in Reutlingen oder an einer der Partnerhoch-
schulen
- Gemeinsames Master-Programm mit der Lancaster University
- Wissenschaftliche und praktische Konzepte

Corporate Relations: Wir denken weiter

- Corporate MBA
- Unternehmensberatung
- Sponsoren
- Career Center

www.esb-reutlingen.de

ibidem-Verlag
Melchiorstr. 15
D-70439 Stuttgart

info@ibidem-verlag.de

www.ibidem-verlag.de
www.edition-noema.de
www.autorenbetreuung.de